Everyman's Poetry

Everyman, I will go with thee,
and be thy guide

Jane Austen: Poems and Favourite Poems

Selected and edited by DOUGLAS BROOKS-DAVIES

EVERYMAN
J. M. Dent · London

This edition first published in Everyman Paperbacks in 1998
Selection, Introduction and other critical apparatus
© J. M. Dent 1998

J. M. Dent
Orion Publishing Group
Orion House
5 Upper St Martin's Lane
London WC2H 9EA

Typeset by Deltatype Ltd, Birkenhead, Merseyside
Printed in Great Britain by
The Guernsey Press Co. Ltd, Guernsey, C. I.

British Library Cataloguing-in-Publication
Data is available on request

ISBN 0 460 87959 6

Juvenilia, 'My dearest Frank', 'I've a Pain in my Head', 'When Stretched on
One's Bed' and 'Written at Winchester on Tuesday the 15th July 1817'
reprinted by kind permission of Oxford University Press
'Lines written by Jane Austen for . . . a niece . . .' reprinted
by kind permission of Alwyn Austen

Contents

WILLIAM WHITEHEAD

Note on the Author and Editor

JANE AUSTEN was born on 16 December 1775 at Steventon, Hampshire, to the Rev. George Austen and his wife Cassandra. She was the seventh of their eight children, and their second daughter. When she was nine she was sent, with her sister Cassandra, to the Abbey School, Reading, where she stayed a year or so, returning home to be largely taught by her father. She began writing prose and verse parodies and burlesques when she was eleven, and also took part in home threatricals. In 1801 the Austens moved to Bath (which often features in her novels) and, after the death of the Rev. Austen in 1805, to Southampton and, finally, Chawton, near Alton, Hampshire where Jane Austen's brother Edward had inherited an estate. *Sense and Sensibility* was published in 1811, by which time Jane Austen was already revising *Pride and Prejudice* (published 1813) and drafting *Mansfield Park* (1814). She began *Emma* in 1814; by the time it was published in 1815 she had begun *Persuasion* (finished August 1816), which was published with *Northanger Abbey* – revised from the earlier *Susan* also in 1816 – the following year. In May 1817 she moved to Winchester for treatment for an illness that had been evident for some twelve months or so, and was probably Addison's disease. She died on 18 July 1817 and was buried in Winchester Cathedral.

DOUGLAS BROOKS-DAVIES was educated at Merchant Taylors' School, Crosby, and Brasenose College, Oxford. He was Senior Lecturer in English Literature at the University of Manchester until 1993 and is now an Honorary Research Fellow there. The founder editor of Manchester University Press's Literature in Context series, he has published widely on Renaissance, eighteenth and nine-teenth-century English literature. His books include *Number and Pattern in the Eighteenth-Century Novel* (Routledge, 1973); *Pope's 'Dunciad' and the Queen of the Night* (Manchester U. P., 1985); *Oedipal Hamlet* (Macmillan, 1989); and *Dickens's 'Great Expectations': A Critical Study* (Penguin, 1989); his editions include: *Silver Poets of the Sixteenth Century* (1992); *Spenser's 'Fairy Queen'* (1996) (both

Dent); *Spenser; Selected Shorter Poems* (Longman, 1995); and editions of *Alexander Pope* (1996), *Robert Herrick* (1996) and *Four Metaphysical Poets* (1997) for Everyman Poetry. His edition of L. P. Hartley's *The Go-Between* was published by Penguin in 1997.

Chronology of Jane Austen's Life

Year	Age	Life
1775		16 December: Jane Austen born at Steventon, Hants, to the Rev. George Austen and his wife Cassandra (*née* Leigh); she was their seventh child and second daughter
1779	3	23 June: Charles John Austen, the last Austen sibling, born
1782	7	December: performance of *Matilda*, by Thomas Francklin, first amateur play production at Steventon
1783	7	To Oxford, with elder sister Cassandra and cousin Jane Cooper, to be educated by Mrs Ann Cawley (an aunt by marriage). 3 May: the Rev. I. P. G. Lefroy instituted vicar of Ashe, Hants, and moves there. Summer: Mrs Cawley to Southampton; the girls are ill. Edward, Jane's third eldest brother, adopted by distant cousin Thomas Knight II as heir to his estates at Godmersham, Kent, and Chawton and Steventon, Hants
1784	8	July: Sheridan's *The Rivals* performed at Steventon
1785	9–10	Spring: with Cassandra, to the Abbey School, Reading
1786	11	December: the sisters have left school
1787	11–12	Begins to write *Juvenilia*. December: Mrs Centlivre's *The Wonder* performed at Steventon

Chronology of her Times

Year	Artistic Context	Historical Events
1775	Beaumarchais, *Barber of Seville* performed	England hires German mercenaries for American war
1776	Smith, *Wealth of Nations*	American Declaration of Independence
1779	Gluck, *Iphigenia* Johnson, *Lives of the Poets*	First steam mills
1780		The Gordon Riots
1782	Mozart, *The Elopement from the Seraglio*	English lose Minorca; legislative independence for Ireland
1783	Schiller, *Fiesco*	England recognises US; first hot-air balloon voyages
1784	Death of Samuel Johnson Beaumarchais, *Marriage of Figaro*	Parliament dissolved; large majority for Pitt
1785	De Quincey born Cowper, *The Task*	
1786	Burns, *Poems*	Frederick the Great dies; Lord Cornwallis Governor of India; coal-gas used for lighting
1787	Mozart, *Don Giovanni* Schiller, *Don Carlos*; Gluck dies	Miller invents steam-boat

Year	Age	Life
1788	12	January: *The Chances* (Fletcher, adapted Garrick) performed at Steventon. March: Fielding's *Tom Thumb* performed at Steventon. Summer: Jane and Cassandra with parents to Kent and London
1789	13	The Lloyds, mother and daughters, rent parsonage at Deane, Hants
1792	16	January: the Lloyds move to Ibthorpe, Hants. October: Jane and Cassandra visit Lloyds. ?Winter: Cassandra engaged to the Rev. Tom Fowle
1793	17–18	3 June: last *Juvenilia* piece written. December: Jane and Cassandra visit Butler-Harrison cousins at Southampton
1794	18	Summer: Jane and Cassandra visit Leighs at Adlestrop, Glos., and Edward and wife Elizabeth at home at Rowling, Kent. 23 October: death of Thomas Knight II. Autumn: *Lady Susan* may have been written
1795	19–20	Probable composition of *Elinor and Marianne* (prototype of *Sense and Sensibility*). Autumn: Rev. Tom Fowle made chaplain to Lord Craven. December: Tom Lefroy visits Ashe
1796	20	January: Tom Lefroy to London; Rev. Tom Fowle to West Indies with Lord Craven. April: Jane and Cassandra visit Cooper family at Harpsden, Oxon. August: taken by brothers Edward and Frank to London and Rowling. September/October: back at Steventon; begins *First Impressions* (prototype of *Pride and Prejudice*)
1797	21	February: death of Tom Fowle. August: *First Impressions* completed. 1 November: Mr Austen sends *First Impressions* to publisher Cadell, who

Year	Artistic Context	Historical Events
1788	Byron born Gainsborough dics	First issue of *The Times*; Bonnie Prince Charlie dies
1789	Blake, *Songs of Innocence*	Fall of Bastille: French Revolution; George Washington US president
1790	Burke: *Reflections on the Revolution in France*	
1791	Paine, *Rights of Man* Boswell, *Life of Johnson*	Anti-Jacobin riots
1792	Wollstonecraft, *Rights of Woman*	French Republic established
1793	Godwin, *Political Justice* Wordsworth, *Descriptive Sketches*	Louis XVI and Marie Antoinette guillotined; France declares war on England; Reign of Terror
1794	Blake, *Songs of Experience* Radcliffe, *Udolpho* Paine, *Age of Reason*	Robespierre executed; Terror ends; habeas corpus suspended
1795	Keats, Carlyle born Lewis, *The Monk* Goethe, *Wilhelm Meister*	Speenhamland Act (Poor Law): wages supplemented by doles
1796	Robert Burns dies Haydn, 'Emperor' Quartet	Jenner's first vaccination
1797	Radcliffe, *The Italian* *Anti-Jacobin* begins	Bank of England suspends cash payments; England begins iron exports

Year	Age	Life
1797		rejects it; work on revising *Elinor and Marianne* into *Sense and Sensibility* begins; with Mrs Austen and Cassandra to Leigh-Pierrot family at Bath; Edward moves with family to Godmersham
1798	22	August: with Cassandra and parents to Godmersham; may have started *Susan* (prototype of *Northanger Abbey*). 24 October: returns to Steventon
1799	23	17 May: with Mrs Austen to 13 Queen Square, Bath. June: home to Steventon; *Susan* probably completed. Late summer: various family visits
1800	24–5	November–December: visits Lloyds at Ibthorpe; the Rev. Austen decides to retire to Bath
1801	25	May: the Austen family leave Steventon and lease 4 Sydney Place, Bath; a Devon holiday follows and (according to tradition) Jane's 'west country romance' may have occurred between now and 1804
1802	26–7	Summer: another Devon holiday, followed by various family visits. Winter: revision of *Susan*
1803	27	Spring: *Susan* sold to London publisher, Crosby and Co., for £10. November: the Austens visit Lyme Regis
1804	28	*The Watsons* written. Spring: Mrs Austen ill. Summer: another family visit to Lyme Regis. 25 October: the Austens move to 3 Green Park Buildings East, Bath. 16 December: Madam Anne Lefroy of Ashe killed in riding accident
1805	29	21 January: death of Rev. Austen at Bath. 25 March: Mrs Austen and daughters move to 25 Gay Street, Bath. 16 April: death of Mrs Lloyd of Ibthorpe; daughter Martha joins Austens. September–November: Mrs Austen and daughters and Martha at Worthing

Year	Artistic Context	Historical Events
1798	Wordsworth and Coleridge, *Lyrical Ballads* Malthus, *Essay on the Principles of Population*	Bonaparte invades Egypt: Battle of the Nile
1799	Thomas Campbell, *The Pleasures of Hope*	Pitt introduces income tax (abolished 1802); Bonaparte made First Consul after *coup d'état*
1800	Burns, *Works* Schiller, *Mary Stuart* Beethoven, First Symphony	Act of Union (Great Britain and Ireland) Bill passed
1801	Southey, *Thalaba* Haydn, *The Seasons*	French leave Egypt (returned to Turkey); Elgin Marbles to London
1802	Scott, *Minstrelsy of the Scottish Border*, vols I, II	Bonaparte appointed Consul for life; law against child labour in England
1803	Scott, *Minstrelsy of the Scottish Border*, vol III	War declared against France; Louisiana bought by US from France
1804	Schiller, *William Tell*	Bonaparte crowned emperor as Napoleon I
1805	Scott, *Lay of the Last Minstrel* Wordsworth, *The Prelude* Beethoven, *Fidelio* Schiller dies	21 October: Battle of Trafalgar

Year	Age	Life
1806	30	2 July: Mrs Austen and daughters leave Bath for Adlestrop
1807	31	March: the Austens move to Southampton
1808	32–3	Various family visits
1809	33	5 April: attempts to push publication of *Susan* unsuccessful. 7 July: Mrs Austen and daughters move into Chawton Cottage on Edward's estate
1810	34–5	Winter: *Sense and Sensibility* accepted for publication
1811	35–6	February: begins *Mansfield Park*. March: corrects proofs of *Sense and Sensibility*. 30 October: *Sense and Sensibility* published by T. Egerton of Whitehall. ?Winter: begins revision of *First Impressions* into *Pride and Prejudice*
1812	36	November: sells copyright of *Pride and Prejudice* to Egerton for £110
1813	37	28 January: *Pride and Prejudice* published. April, May: visits London. ?July: completes *Mansfield Park*. 17 August: Anna Austen and Ben Lefroy engaged. November: *Mansfield Park* accepted by Egerton
1814	38–9	21 January: begins *Emma*. 9 May: *Mansfield Park* published. 8 November: marriage of Anna Austen and Ben Lefroy. 26 December: with Cassandra stays with Mrs Heathcote and Miss Bigg in Winchester

Year	Artistic Context	Historical Events
1806	Beethoven, 'Appassionata' piano sonata	Pitt dies; English blockade French coast; British occupy Cape of Good Hope
1807	Charles and Mary Lamb, *Tales from Shakespeare* Crabbe, *Parish Register* Moore, *Irish Melodies*	Slave trade abolished in British Empire; Peninsular War begins
1808	Scott, *Marmion* Goethe, *Faust*, Part I Beethoven, Fifth Symphony	Napoleon invades Spain
1809	Byron, *English Bards and Scotch Reviewers* Campbell, *Gertrude of Wyoming* *Quarterly Review* founded	Napoleon captures Vienna; Sir John Moore killed at Corunna.
1810	Scott, *Lady of the Lake* Crabbe, *The Borough*	George III now recognised as insane
1811	Shelley, *Necessity of Atheism*	Prince of Wales made regent (Regency Bill); Luddite uprisings begin
1812	Byron, *Childe Harold*, I and II Grimm, *Fairy Tales*	Napoleon invades Russia; retreat from Moscow
1813	Shelley, *Queen Mab* Byron, *Giaour* and *Bride of Abydos* Southey poet laureate	Wellington enters France; Colombia, Uruguay, Chile break away from Spain
1814	Fanny Burney, *The Wanderer* Scott, *Waverley* Byron, *The Corsair, Lara* Southey, *Vision of Judgement* Wordsworth, *Excursion*	First effective steam locomotive (Stephenson); Pius VII restores Inquisition; 5 April: Napoleon abdicates; exiled to Elba

1815	39–40	29 March: completes *Emma*. 8 August: begins *Persuasion*; in London to negotiate terms for *Emma*'s publication. Late December: publication of *Emma* by John Murray
1816	40	Spring: begins to feel unwell; revises *Susan* (bought back from Crosby and Co.) into *Northanger Abbey*. 18 July: completes first draft of *Persuasion*. 6 August: finishes *Persuasion*
1817	41	27 January: begins *Sanditon*. 18 March: stops work on *Sanditon*. 28 March: makes will. 24 May: with Cassandra to 8 College Street, Winchester. 18 July: death of Jane Austen. 24 July: burial in Winchester Cathedral. End December: *Northanger Abbey* and *Persuasion* published together by John Murray in 4 volumes

Year	Artistic Context	Historical Events
1815	Scott, *Guy Mannering* Byron, *Hebrew Melodies* Canova's Three Graces sculpture	March: Napoleon escapes and returns to France; hostilities resumed; 18 June: Battle of Waterloo ends French war
1816	Shelley, *Alastor and Other Poems* Byron, *Childe Harold*, III Scott, *Old Mortality* Coleridge, 'Kubla Khan'	First protective tariff in US; Spa Fields riot
1817	Byron, *Manfred* Thomas Moore, *Lalla Rookh* Constable's landscapes exhibited Elgin Marbles bought by British Museum	Monroe president of US; treaty with Spain opens trade between West Indies and Britain

Introduction

Most of us know only Jane Austen the novelist: the satirical, ironical and humorous teller of tales about folly and common sense, self-deception and self-knowledge; the miniaturist of a privileged class and a lost rural economy. But if we want the woman behind the public mask, we should go to the letters and the poems. There aren't, in fact, many of the latter – some twenty or so – and yet, although her mother was the acknowledged poet of the family, Jane Austen's own poems, some included in letters, some just thrown off at the slightest whim, reveal a humour, controlled bathos, humanity and pathos that many may feel (perhaps unjustly) is often missing from the novels.

The few verse burlesques from the *Juvenilia* (*c.* 1787–93) reveal a sure awareness of current conventions and of their intrinsic silliness: the pastoral love poem with its Strephons and Chloes; the apparatus of the voguish melancholic ode, which she neatly parodies and deflates with zeugma in 'I delight to tread/The paths of honour and the myrtle grove' (compare 'Gently brawling down the turnpike road,/Sweetly noisy falls the silent stream'; both from the 'Ode to Pity'). Or there's the genuine sense of caught conversation in 'How d'ye do, my Uncle Francis?/How does do your lady dear?' (the last lines of 'Lines written . . . for the amusement of a niece') and 'Oh! Mr Best, you're very bad', the latter introducing us to Jane Austen's ready sense of the wit to be elicited from names, which we see as well in 'On . . . the Marriage of "Mr Gell . . . to Miss Gill" ' and 'On the Marriage of Miss Camilla Wallop . . .'. There is even – surprisingly to those who thought that Jane Austen was unaware of anything that went on outside Chawton and Godmersham, Highbury and Netherfield – a verse on a public theme, the court martial of Sir Home Popham in 1807; although, of course, it is the private world that predominates in these essentially ephemeral pieces. Nevertheless, however transient the original experience was, it is moving and rather warming to find ourselves sharing a headache with the novelist, and with it that ancient recognition that we can think straight only when we are well ('When Stretched on One's Bed').

Less ephemeral, however, is the grieving self of the elegy, written four years after the event, commemorating the death of Anne Lefroy on Jane Austen's birthday in 1804. Starting with formal diction and compliment, it soon becomes something more when Anne Lefroy – to whom Jane Austen had been quite close – appears as a vision, conjured by the elegist's words and the intensity of her thought in a way that will be familiar to most of us who have lost close loved ones. It perhaps stumbles as a poem: the words remain stilted, the piety a bit too conventional. Yet it is the stiltedness that we have all achieved when we have tried to write down our feelings about a dead relative or friend; and we value the glimpse it gives us into a private moment while at the same time feeling that we should not have peeped so far. That feeling deepens when we read the amusing and kindly poem evoking the ghost of St Swithin and his gift of rain to the July race-meeting at Winchester ('Written at Winchester . . .'). Jane Austen wrote it in a moment's respite from her last illness only three days before she died, and, as she knew how ill she was, the showers presumably also represent the rain that should, according to tradition, bless the dead.

In date the poems cover all of Jane Austen's writing life, and this volume prints them all. It also includes a further glimpse into her imaginative world by printing generous excerpts from the poems that she is known to have read and valued. These are the poems mentioned or quoted in her letters and novels (Shakespeare has been omitted because her several references are only to the plays, as has the poet dramatist William Hayley, whom she is known to have read but to whom she makes no reference; omitted, too, are the songs she copied into her manuscript notebook, 'Songs and Duets', again because they make no impact on her written work). Several of the poets who are represented here and were formerly well known have faded almost completely from our collective memory: James Beattie, Thomas Campbell, even Crabbe (except for his influence on Benjamin Britten), Cowper, Southey and Scott. Others were very minor even in their own day: James Merrick, for example, or William Whitehead. Nevertheless, in recapturing their words we are not only testing the parameters of Jane Austen's poetic taste – it is, at the very least, interesting to see which bits stuck in her mind and were mentioned later – but, in addition, exploring the literature that she often devoured as soon as it was published. Alongside the novels that she read with such gusto, it is touching, for instance, to read in her letter of 24 January 1817 how promptly she had seized on Southey's *Poet's Pilgrimage to Waterloo* (1816), and how admiring she was of its proem. Southey's love for his son struck her particularly; and her response somehow reflects back on the earlier and understated emotions of the elegy for Mrs Lefroy to remind us that Jane Austen's novels express certain aspects of her mind only: others, the emotional, the sentimental, she kept firmly under control, to release them, on occasion only, into her poems and correspondence.

Yet is this to misread the novels slightly? When, in *Persuasion*, Jane Austen makes Captain Benwick mention Byron and Scott so often it is primarily to characterise him as a victim of his feelings, to raise a question over the dependability of a man who immerses himself so unhealthily in Middle Eastern tales of revenge and unsatisfied love, and in quasi-medieval Border romances. He is also, like Sir Edward in *Sanditon* – a man even more afflicted with the demon of quotations on the tip of the tongue – a social bore. Yet Jane Austen relished these very verses herself. The novels that quote them, or refer to them, use them in a formal, allusive sense, with the aim of delineating character or teasing out ironies (we shall look at more examples in a moment); but they also *contain* them as voices from beyond the world of the novel – and from Jane Austen's darker imaginative self – telling of the alternative realities of murder, Catholic confession, unquiet souls, wizardry – even politics. After all, Scott had a political purpose in reinventing (and inventing) Scots mythology and legend. It might not have been very real to a woman writing in Hampshire but, like the London riots in *Northanger Abbey* (I.14) that exist simply because they are mentioned, the eruptions of Scott and Byron (not to mention Burns, and Garrick's slightly obscene little riddle in *Emma*) into her fictions inevitably carry their own message, and it is one that runs counter to the novels' overt meanings.

Scott reappears in *Mansfield Park* (I.9) when Fanny, disappointed at the simple sobriety of Sotherton chapel, invokes *The Lady of the Lake* and the tomb of a dead Scottish king as the kind of thing she had been hoping to see. Her quotation suggests a 'gothick' depth which we perhaps had not expected from this mouse of a heroine. It speaks, too, beyond its immediate location in the text, of the complacent sense of identity enjoyed by the English squirearchy in contrast to the turmoil of Scots nationalistic aspirations. Similarly, Fanny's invocation of Cowper's *The Task*, Book I, on being told of the possibility of the cutting down of the avenue at Sotherton, endows her with a sensitivity that we might not have expected (*Mansfield Park*, I.6). The quotation is, in addition, a neat example of Jane Austen's allusive wit; for, as we see from the excerpt in the present volume, Fanny's lines appear in a context of closed gates willingly opened by their owner, and a permitted walk in the estate's wilderness. In contrast, when the visit to Sotherton finally takes place, Henry Crawford and Miss Bertram, impatient of waiting for the owner, Rushworth, and the key that will open the gate to the park and wilderness, force their way through, unable to stand the restraint. It is a minor act of impatience and ill manners, but the greater when seen in terms of the decorums observed in the lines by Cowper, Jane Austen's favourite moralist.

Again in *Mansfield Park* (3.14), the quotation from Cowper's *Tirocinium* is more than just a way of underlining Fanny's homesickness, for it opens up several ironies when we know that the poem is about the advantages of home tuition with a sympathetic parent and that Fanny recalls Cowper's line because she feels so completely alien at her parental home in Portsmouth, realising how real a home Mansfield Park has become for her. And the poem's questions about true homes and parents who do not have authority over, or the love of, their children implicate Sir Thomas Bertram and his adequacy as a father, a matter central to the whole novel.

Equally complex is the mention of Crabbe in *Mansfield Park* (I.16). Fanny has a copy of the *Tales* on the table in the white attic, along with the *Idler* and Lord Macartney's *Journal of the Embassy to China*. Whatever she may have intended to get in terms of edification and information from the last two, the mention of one of her favourite cautionary poets' *Tales* seems to point firmly to 'Tale 11, Edward Shore.' I have excerpted part of that tale in this volume to give the flavour of Crabbe to those who are unacquainted with him and because of its appropriateness to Fanny's perception of Edmund at this moment: apparently upright, yet yielding (like his near namesake in the tale) to the treachery of temptation and the betrayal of principle. If we agree that this tale does indeed hover at the back of Fanny's mind, then we also appreciate Jane Austen's kindly irony at her naïve heroine's expense: life isn't as easy as moral fables suggest; one difficult and perhaps wrong decision on Edmund's part doesn't mean that he is on the path to lunacy like Edward Shore.

Also worth looking at is Henry Crawford's quotation of a line from Milton's *Paradise Lost*, 5 in *Mansfield Park* (I.4): 'I am of a cautious temper, and unwilling to risk my happiness in a hurry. Nobody can think more highly of the matrimonial state than myself. I consider the blessing of a wife as most justly described in those discreet lines of the poet, "Heaven's *last* best gift".' This is superficially a joke at the expense of wives uttered by a frivolous man about town who has no intention of settling down until he has played the field, yet it works against him because the context of the line is Eve's disturbed sleep after a seductive, dreamlike temptation from Satan disguised as an angelic youth; so that Henry's joke carries with it the freight of the corrupting threat that the Crawfords embody in respect of Fanny and Mansfield Park as a whole.

Not all allusions in the novels carry such weight, of course. Mrs Elton's reference to 'Hymen's saffron robe' in connection with her husband's courtship of her (*Emma*, II.18), for example, is a quote from Milton's *L'Allegro* that had become something of a commonplace: it is a tag like her 'caro sposo', pretentious and embarrassing. Similarly, when, in *Emma* (II.15), she quotes from Gray's *Elegy*, it means very little, whereas when the same lines are quoted in connection with Catherine Morland's training as a heroine in the first chapter of *Northanger Abbey*, they say quite a lot about the desire to escape from a limiting background, and the sadness of lost opportunity.

I hope that the poems and excerpts from poems printed in this anthology will enable readers to pursue similar speculations for themselves and, above all, that they offer an insight into an often neglected aspect of Jane Austen's own writing and reading. Some readers may be struck by apparently surprising omissions: of Wordsworth, for instance, or Coleridge. But there is no hint that Jane Austen read Coleridge, and the one mention of Wordsworth – by Sir Edward in *Sanditon*, chapter 7 ('Montgomery has all the fire of poetry, Wordsworth has the true soul of it') – doesn't tell us enough for us even to begin to guess which Wordsworth poems Jane Austen might have come across. Besides, we can all get hold of a Wordsworth, but James Beattie and James Merrick are a different matter.

DOUGLAS BROOKS-DAVIES

Note on the Text

Jane Austen's poems are mainly found in her *Juvenilia* and letters. The texts in the present edition follow, for the most part, those in *The Works of Jane Austen*, vol. VI, *Minor Works*, revised B. C. Southam (London, New York, Toronto: Oxford University Press, 1969). Spelling and punctuation have been modernised.

The interested reader is recommended also to consult *Jane Austen's Letters*, ed. Deirdre Le Faye, 3rd edition (Oxford, New York; Oxford University Press, 1995) and *Jane Austen: Collected Poems and Verse of the Austen Family*, ed. David Selwyn (Manchester: Carcanet, 1996).

Texts of all other works anthologised in this edition are either from first editions or from editions available in Jane Austen's lifetime. Spelling and punctuation have again been modernised, with the exception of geographical names in Scott's poems, and the retention of conscious archaisms (e.g., 'ladye' in Scott's *The Lay of the Last Minstrel*).

Jane Austen

Song (1)

That Damon was in love with me
    I once thought and believed;
But now that he is not I see,
    I fear I was deceived.

Epitaph

Here lies our friend who, having promis–ed
That unto two she would be marri-ed,
Threw her sweet body and her lovely face
Into the stream that runs through Portland Place.

Song (2)

When Corydon went to the fair
    He bought a red ribbon for Bess,
With which she encircled her hair
    And made herself look very fess.

Song

Though misfortunes my footsteps may ever attend,
    I hope I shall never have need of a friend,
As an innocent heart I will ever preserve
    And will never from Virtue's dear boundaries swerve.

To Miss Austen, the following Ode to Pity is dedicated, from a thorough
knowledge of her pitiful nature, by her obedient humble servant, The Author

Ode to Pity

1

Ever musing, I delight to tread
   The paths of honour and the myrtle grove,
Whilst the pale Moon her beams doth shed
      On disappointed love,
While Philomel on airy hawthorn bush   5
   Sings sweet and melancholy, and the thrush
Converses with the dove.

2

Gently brawling down the turnpike road,
   Sweetly noisy falls the silent stream –
The Moon emerges from behind a cloud   10
   And darts upon the myrtle grove her beam.
Ah! then what lovely scenes appear:
   The hut, the cot, the grot, and chapel queer,
And eke the abbey, too, in mouldering heap,
   Concealed by aged pines, her head doth rear   15
And, quite invisible, doth take a peep.

Song (1)

Chloe]   I go to Town,
          And when I come down
          I shall be married to Streephon,
          And that to me will be fun.
Chorus]   Be fun, be fun, be fun,   5
             And that to me will be fun.

Song (2)

Chloe]   I am going to have my dinner,
          After which I shan't be thinner.
          I wish I had here Streephon,
          For he would carve the partridge
             if it should be a tough one.
Chorus]   Tough one, tough one, tough one,   5
             For he would carve the partridge if it should
               be a tough one.

'This Little Bag'

This little bag I hope will prove
   To be not vainly made.
For, if you thread and needle want,
   It will afford you aid.

And, as we are about to part,   5
   'Twill serve another end,
For when you look upon the bag
   You'll recollect your friend.

Lines written by Jane Austen for the amusement of a niece (afterwards Lady Knatchbull) or the arrival of Captain and Mrs Austen at Godmersham Park after their marriage July 1806

See, they come post haste from Thanet,
   Lovely couple, side by side;
They've left behind them Richard Kennet
   With the parents of the bride!

Canterbury they have passed through;   5
   Next succeeded Stamford Bridge;
Chilham village they came fast through;
   Now they've mounted yonder ridge.

Down the hill they're swift proceeding;
   Now they skirt the Park around;   10
Lo! the cattle, sweetly feeding,
   Scamper, startled, at the sound!

Run, my brothers, to the pier gate!
   Throw it open very wide!
Let it not be said that we're late   15
   In welcoming my uncle's bride!

To the house the chaise advances;
   Now it stops – they're here, they're here!
'How d'ye do, my Uncle Francis?
   'How does do your lady dear?'   20

'Oh! Mr Best, you're very bad'

Oh! Mr Best, you're very bad,
   And all the world shall know it;
Your base behaviour shall be sung
   By me, a tuneful poet:

You used to go to Harrogate   5
   Each summer as it came,
And why, I pray, should you refuse
   To go this year the same?

The way's as plain, the road's as smooth,
   The posting not increased;   10
You're scarcely stouter than you were,
   Not younger, sir, at least.

If e'er the waters were of use,
   Why now their use forego?
You may not live another year –   15
   All's mortal here below.

It is your duty, Mr Best,
   To give your health repair:
Vain else your Richard's pills will be,
   And vain your consort's care.   20

But yet a nobler duty calls
   You now towards the North:
Arise ennobled – as escort
   Of Martha Lloyd, stand forth.

She wants your aid – she honours you   25
   With a distinguished call.
Stand forth to be the friend of her
   Who is the friend of all –

Take her, and wonder at your luck
    In having such a trust: 30
Her converse sensible and sweet
    Will banish heat and dust.

So short she'll make the journey seem,
    You'll bid the chaise stand still:
'Twill be like driving at full speed   35
    From Newbury to Speen Hill.

Convey her safe to Morton's wife
    And I'll forget the past,
And write some verses in your praise
    As finely and as fast.   40

But if you still refuse to go,
    I'll never let you rest,
But haunt you with reproachful song,
    O wicked Mr Best!

On Sir Home Popham's sentence – April 1807

Of a Ministry pitiful, angry, mean,
A gallant commander the victim is seen:
For promptitude, vigour, success, does he stand
Condemned to receive a severe reprimand!
To his foes I could wish a resemblance in fate: 5
That they, too, may suffer themselves soon, or late,
The injustice they warrant. But vain is my spite:
They cannot *so* suffer who never do right.

To Miss Bigg,
previous to her marriage,
with some pocket handkerchiefs
I had hemmed for her

Cambric – with grateful blessings would I pay
The pleasure given me in sweet employ;
Long mayest thou serve my friend without decay,
And have no tears to wipe but tears of joy!

On the same occasion, but not sent

Cambric, thou'st been to me a good,
And I would bless thee if I could!
Go, serve thy mistress with delight –
Be small in compass, soft and white:
Enjoy thy fortune, honoured much   5
To bear her name and feel her touch,
And, that thy worth may last for years,
Slight be her colds and few her tears.

To the Memory of Mrs Lefroy,
who died December 16 – my birthday –
written 1808

The day returns again, my natal day:
What mixed emotions in my mind arise!
Beloved friend, four years have passed away
Since thou wert snatched forever from our eyes.

The day commemorative of my birth,   5
Bestowing life and light and hope to me,
Brings back the hour which was thy last on earth:
Oh bitter pang of torturing memory!

Angelic woman, past my power to praise
In language meet thy talents, temper, mind,   10
Thy solid worth, thy captivating grace! –
Thou friend and ornament of humankind!

At Johnson's death by Hamilton 'twas said,
'Seek we a substitute – ah, vain the plan! –
No second best remains to Johnson dead: 15
None can remind us even of the man'.

So we of thee – unequalled in thy race;
Unequalled thou, as he the first of men.
Vainly we search around thy vacant place:
We ne'er may look upon the like again.   20

But come, fond Fancy, thou indulgent power:
Hope is desponding, chill, severe to thee!
Bless thou this little portion of an hour:
Let me behold her as she used to be.

I see her here, with all her smiles benign,   25
Her looks of eager love, her accents sweet;
That voice and coutenance almost divine;
Expression, harmony, alike complete.

Listen: 'tis not sound alone – 'tis sense,
'Tis genius, taste, and tenderness of soul: 30
'Tis genuine warmth of heart without pretence,
And purity of mind that crowns the whole.

She speaks! 'Tis eloquence – that grace of tongue
So rare, so lovely, never misapplied
By her to palliate vice or deck a wrong: 35
She speaks and argues but on virtue's side.

Hers is the energy of soul sincere:
Her Christian spirit, ignorant to feign,
Seeks but to comfort, heal, enlighten, cheer,
Confer a pleasure or prevent a pain.   40

Can aught enhance such goodness? Yes – to me
Her partial favour from my earliest years
Consummates all. Ah, give me yet to see
Her smile of love – the vision disappears.

'Tis past and gone: we meet no more below;   45
Short is the cheat of Fancy o'er the tomb.
Oh might I hope to equal bliss to go,
To meet thee, angel, in thy future home!

Fain would I feel an union in thy fate,
Fain would I seek to draw an omen fair   50
From this connection in our earthly date:
Indulge the harmless weakness, Reason – spare . . .

'Alas, poor Brag, thou boastful Game'

'Alas, poor brag, thou boastful game! What now avails
            thine empty name?
Where now thy more distinguished fame? – My day is o'er,
            and thine the same,
For thou, like me, art thrown aside at Godmersham this
            Christmas tide.
And now, across the table wide, each game (save brag
            or spec) is tried':
Such is the mild ejaculation of tender-hearted   5
            speculation.

'My dearest Frank'

My dearest Frank, I wish you joy
Of Mary's safety with a boy,
Whose birth has given little pain
Compared with that of Mary Jane.
May he a growing blessing prove,   5
And well deserve his parents' love,
Endowed with Art's and Nature's good,
Thy name possessing, with thy blood:
In him, in all his ways, may we
Another Francis William see!   10
Thy infant ways may he inherit,
Thy warmth – nay insolence – of spirit:
We would not with one fault dispense
To weaken the resemblance.
May he revive thy nursery sin,   15
Peeping as daringly within
(His curly locks but just descried),
With 'Bet, my be not come to bide'.

Fearless of danger, braving pain,
And threatened very oft in vain,   20
Still may one terror daunt his soul,
One needful engine of control
Be found in this sublime array,
A neighbouring donkey's awful bray! –
So may his equal faults as child   25
Produce maturity as mild:
His saucy words and fiery ways
In early childhood's pettish days
In manhood show his father's mind,
Like him considerate and kind –   30
All gentleness to those around,
And eager only not to wound.

Then, like his father too, he must,
To his own former struggles just,

Feel his deserts with honest glow,   35
And all his self-improvement know:
A native fault may thus give birth
To the best blessing, conscious worth.

As for ourselves – we're very well,
As unaffected prose will tell.   40
Cassandra's pen will paint our state,
The many comforts that await
Our Chawton home – how much we find
Already in it to our mind,
And how convinced that, when complete,   45
It will all other houses beat
That ever have been made or mended,
With rooms concise or rooms distended.
You'll find us very snug next year,
Perhaps with Charles and Fanny near –   50
For now it often does delight us
To fancy them just over-right us.

'In Measured Verse . . .'

In measured verse I'll now rehearse
   The charms of lovely Anna:
And first, her mind is unconfined,
   Like any vast savannah.

Ontario's lake may fitly speak   5
   Her fancy's ample bound:
Its circuit may, on strict survey,
   Five hundred miles be found.

Her wit descends on foes and friends
   Like famed Niagara's Fall;   10
And travellers gaze in wild amaze,
   And listen one and all.

Her judgement sound, thick, black, profound,
   Like transatlantic groves,
Dispenses aid and friendly shade   15
   To all that in it roves.

If thus her mind to be defined
   America exhausts,
And all that's grand in that great land
   In similes it costs –   20

Oh, how can I her person try
   To image and portray?
How paint the face, the form how trace
   In which those virtues lay?

Another world must be unfurled,   25
   Another language known,
Ere tongue or sound can publish round
   Her charms of flesh and bone.

'I've a Pain in my Head'

'I've a pain in my head,'
   Said the suffering Beckford
To her doctor so dread:
   'Ah! what shall I take for't?'

Said her doctor so dread,   5
   Whose name it was Newnham,
'For this pain in your head,
   Ah! what can you do, ma'am?'

Said Miss Beckford: 'Suppose –
   If you think there's no risk –   10

I take a good dose
   Of calomel brisk?'

'What a praiseworthy notion!',
   Replied Mr Newnham:
'You shall have such a potion,   15
   And so will I, too, ma'am.'

On Reading in the Newspaper, the Marriage of 'Mr Gell of Eastbourne to Miss Gill'

Of Eastbourne, Mr Gell,
   From being perfectly well,
Became dreadfully ill
   For the love of Miss Gill.

So he said, with some sighs,   5
   'I'm the slave of your *eyes* –
Ah! restore, if you please,
   By accepting my *ease*'.

'I am in a Dilemma'

'I am in a dilemma, for want of an Emma,'
Escaped from the lips of Henry Gipps.

'Between Session and Session'

Between session and session
The first prepossession
May rouse up the nation
And the villainous bill
May be forced to lie still   5
Against wicked men's will.

'When Stretched on One's Bed'

When stretched on one's bed
With a fierce throbbing head
Which precludes alike thought or repose,
How little one cares
For the grandest affairs   5
That may busy the world as it goes!

How little one feels
For the waltzes and reels
Of our dance-loving friends at a ball;
How slight one's concern   10
To conjecture or learn
What their flounces or hearts may befall!

How little one minds
If a company dines
On the best that the season affords;   15
How short is one's Muse
O'er the sauces and stews,
Or the guests, be they beggars or lords!

How little the bells –
Ring they peels, toll they knells –   20
Can attract our attention or ears:

The bride may be married,
The corse may be carried,
And touch nor our hopes nor our fears!

Our own bodily pains   25
Every faculty chains –
We can feel on no subject beside!
'Tis in health and in ease
We the power must seize
For our friends and our souls to provide.   30

On the Marriage of Miss Camilla Wallop and the Reverend Wake

Camilla, good-humoured, and merry, and small,
For a husband was at her last stake;
And having in vain danced at many a ball
Is now happy to jump at a Wake.

Riddles

When my first is a task to a young girl of spirit,
And my second confines her to finish the piece,
How hard is her fate! But how great is her merit
If, by taking my whole, she effect her release!

Divided, I'm a gentleman
In public deeds and powers;
United, I'm a monster who oft
That gentleman devours.

You may lie on my first, by the side of a stream,
And my second compose to the nymph you adore;
But if, when you've none of my whole, her esteem
And affection diminish, think of her no more.

To Miss—.
Charade

My first displays the wealth and pomp of kings,
    Lords of the earth, their luxury and ease.
Another view of man my second brings –
    Behold him there, the monarch of the seas!

But, ah, united, what reverse we have!   5
    Man's boasted power and freedom – all are flown:
Lord of the earth and sea, he bends, a slave,
    And woman, lovely woman, reigns alone.

    Thy ready wit the word will soon supply:
    May its approval beam in that soft eye!   10

Written at Winchester on Tuesday
the 15th July 1817

When Winchester races first took their beginning,
It is said the good people forgot their old saint,
Not applying at all for the leave of St Swithin,
And that William of Wykeham's approval was faint.

The races, however, were fixed and determined: 5
The company met and the weather was charming;

The lords and the ladies were satined and ermined,
And nobody saw any future alarming.

But when the old saint was informed of these doings,
He made but one spring from his shrine to the roof   10
Of the palace which now lies so sadly in ruins,
And thus he addressed them all, standing aloof:

'O subjects rebellious, O Venta depraved –
When once we are buried you think we are dead,
But behold me immortal. By vice you're enslaved: 15
You have sinned and must suffer.' Then further he said:

'These races and revels and dissolute measures
With which you're debasing a neighbouring plain –
Let them stand: you shall meet with your curse in your
   pleasures;
Set off for your course, I'll pursue with my rain.   20

'Ye cannot but know my command in July:
Henceforward I'll triumph in showing my powers –
Shift your race as you will, it shall never be dry;
The curse upon Venta is July in showers.'

JAMES BEATTIE

The Hermit

At the close of day, when the hamlet is still,
And mortals the sweets of forgetfulness prove,
When naught but the torrent is heard on the hill,
And naught but the nightingale's song in the grove:
'Twas thus, by the cave of the mountain afar,   5
While his harp rung symphonious, a hermit began;
No more with himself or with nature at war,
He thought as a sage, though he felt as a man:

'Ah! why, all abandoned to darkness and woe,
Why, lone Philomela, that languishing fall?   10
For spring shall return, and a lover bestow,
And sorrow no longer thy bosom enthrall.
But if pity inspire thee, renew the sad lay,
Mourn, sweetest complainer, man calls thee to mourn;
Oh soothe him, whose pleasures, like thine, pass away: 15
Full quickly they pass – but they never return.

'Now gliding remote, on the verge of the sky,
The Moon half-extinguished her crescent displays:
But lately I marked, when majestic on high
She shone, and the planets were lost in her blaze.   20
Roll on, thou fair orb, and with gladness pursue
The path that conducts thee to splendour again:
But man's faded glory what change shall renew?
Ah, fool! to exult in a glory so vain!

''Tis night, and the landscape is lovely no more: 25
I mourn, but, ye woodlands, I mourn not for you;
For morn is approaching, your charms to restore,
Perfumed with fresh fragrance, and glittering with dew;
Nor yet for the ravage of winter I mourn;
Kind Nature the embryo blossom will save: 30
But when shall spring visit the mouldering urn?
Oh when shall it dawn on the night of the grave?

''Twas thus, by the glare of false science betrayed,
That leads, to bewilder, and dazzles, to blind,
My thoughts wont to roam, from shade onward to shade,   35
Destruction before me, and sorrow behind.
"O pity, great Father of light," then I cried,
"Thy creature, who fain would not wander from Thee;
Lo, humbled in dust, I relinquish my pride:
From doubt and from darkness Thou only canst free."   40

'And darkness and doubt are now flying away;
No longer I roam in conjecture forlorn.

So breaks on the traveller, faint, and astray,
The bright and the balmy effulgence of morn.
See Truth, Love, and Mercy, in triumph descending,   45
And nature all glowing in Eden's first bloom!
On the cold cheek of Death smiles and roses are blending,
And Beauty immortal awakes from the tomb.'

ISAAC HAWKINS BROWNE

from A Pipe of Tobacco: In Imitation of Six Several Authors

IMITATION 5

Blest leaf! whose aromatic gales dispense
To templars modesty, to parsons sense:
So raptured priests, at famed Dodona's shrine,
Drank inspiration from the steam divine.
Poison that cures, a vapour that affords   5
Content more solid than the smile of lords:
Rest to the weary, to the hungry food,
The last kind refuge of the wise and good.
Inspired by thee, dull cits adjust the scale
Of Europe's peace when other statesmen fail.   10
By thee protected, and thy sister, beer,
Poets rejoice, nor think the bailiff near.
Nor less the critic owns thy genial aid,
While supperless he plies the piddling trade.
What though to love and soft delights a foe,   15
By ladies hated, hated by the beau,
Yet social freedom, long to courts unknown,
Fair health, fair truth, and virtue are thy own:
Come to thy poet, come with healing wings,
And let me taste thee, unexcised by kings.   20

ROBERT BURNS

Mary Morison

O Mary, at thy window be,
    It is the wished, the trysted hour;
Those smiles and glances let me see
    That make the miser's treasure poor:
How blithely wad I bide the stour,   5
    A weary slave frae sun to sun,
Could I the rich reward secure,
    The lovely Mary Morison!

Yestreen when, to the trembling string,
    The dance gaed through the lighted ha',   10
To thee my fancy took its wing –
    I sat, but neither heard nor saw:
Though this was fair, and that was braw,
    And yon the toast of a' the town,
I sighed, and said amang them a',   15
    'Ye are na Mary Morison.'

O Mary, canst thou wreck his peace
    Wha for thy sake wad gladly die?
Or canst thou break that heart of his
    Whase only faute is loving thee?   20
If love for love thou wilt na gie,
    At least be pity to me shown:
A thought ungentle canna be
    The thought o' Mary Morison.

Song: Will ye go to the Indies, my Mary

Will ye go to the Indies, my Mary,
   And leave auld Scotia's shore?
Will ye go to the Indies, my Mary,
   Across the Atlantic roar?

Oh sweet grows the lime and the orange,   5
   And the apple on the pine;
But a' the charms o' the Indies
   Can never equal thine.

I hae sworn by the heavens to my Mary,
   I hae sworn by the heavens to be true;   10
And sae may the heavens forget me
   When I forget my vow!

Oh plight me your faith, my Mary,
   And plight me your lily-white hand;
Oh plight me your faith, my Mary,   15
   Before I leave Scotia's strand.

Highland Mary

Ye banks, and braes, and streams around
   The castle o' Montgomery,
Green be your woods, and fair your flowers,
   Your waters never drumlie!
There Simmer first unfald her robes,   5
   And there the langest tarry:
For there I took the last fareweel
   O' my sweet Highland Mary.

How sweetly bloomed the gay, green birk,
   How rich the hawthorn's blossom   10

As, underneath their fragrant shade,
  I clasped her to my bosom!
The golden Hours, on angel wings,
  Flew o'er me and my dearie,
For dear to me as light and life   15
  Was my sweet Highland Mary.

Wi' mony a vow and locked embrace
  Our parting was fu' tender
And, pledging aft to meet again,
  We tore oursels asunder;   20
But oh, fell Death's untimely frost,
  That nipped my flower sae early!
Now green's the sod, and cauld's the clay,
  That wraps my Highland Mary!

Oh pale, pale now, those rosy lips   25
  I aft hae kissed sae fondly!
And closed for ay the sparkling glance
  That dwalt on me sae kindly!
And mouldering now in silent dust
  That heart that lo'ed me dearly!   30
But still within my bosom's core
  Shall live my Highland Mary.

LORD BYRON

from The Giaour: A Fragment of
a Turkish Tale

'And she was lost – and yet I breathed,
  But not the breath of human life:
A serpent round my heart was wreathed,
  And stung my every thought to strife.
Alike all time, abhorred all place,   5

Shuddering I shrunk from Nature's face,
Where every hue that charmed before
The blackness of my bosom wore.
The rest thou dost already know,
And all my sins and half my woe.   10
But talk no more of penitence;
Thou seest I soon shall part from hence;
And if thy holy tale were true,
The deed that's done canst *thou* undo?
Think me not thankless – but this grief   15
Looks not to priesthood for relief.
My soul's estate in secret guess:
But wouldst thou pity more, say less.
When thou canst bid my Leila live,
Then will I sue thee to forgive;   20
Then plead my cause in that high place
Where purchased masses proffer grace.
Go, when the hunter's hand hath wrung
From forest-cave her shrieking young,
And calm the lonely lioness: 25
But soothe not – mock not *my* distress! . . .

'Tell me no more of fancy's gleam,
No, Father, no, 'twas not a dream;
Alas! the dreamer first must sleep, –
I only watched, and wished to weep,   30
But could not, for my burning brow
Throbbed to the very brain as now:
I wished but for a single tear,
As something welcome, new, and dear:
I wished it then, and wish it still;   35
Despair is stronger than my will.
Waste not thine orison, despair
Is mightier than thy pious prayer:
I would not, if I might, be blest;
I want no paradise, but rest.   40
'Twas then, I tell thee, Father! then
I saw her; yes, she lived again;
And shining in her white symar,
As through yon pale grey cloud the star

Which now I gaze on, as on her,   45
Who looked and looks far lovelier;
Dimly I view its trembling spark;
Tomorrow's night shall be more dark;
And I, before its rays appear,
That lifeless thing the living fear.   50
I wander, Father! for my soul
Is fleeting towards its final goal.
I saw her, Friar! and I rose
Forgetful of our former woes;
And rushing from my couch, I dart,   55
And clasp her to my desperate heart;
I clasp – what is it that I clasp?
No breathing form within my grasp,
No heart that beats reply to mine –
Yet, Leila! yet the form is thine!   60
And art thou, dearest, changed so much
As meet my eye, yet mock my touch?
Ah! were thy beauties e'er so cold,
I care not so my arms enfold
The all they ever wished to hold.   65
Alas! around a shadow pressed
They shrink upon my lonely breast;
Yet still 'tis there! in silence stands,
And beckons with beseeching hands!
With braided hair, and bright-black eye –   70
I knew 'twas false – she could not die!
But he is dead! Within the dell
I saw him buried where he fell;
He comes not, for he cannot break
From earth; why then art thou awake?   75
They told me wild waves rolled above
The face I view, the form I love;
They told me – 'twas a hideous tale! –
I'd tell it, but my tongue would fail:
If true, and from thine ocean-cave   80
Thou comest to claim a calmer grave,
Oh pass thy dewy fingers o'er
This brow that then will burn no more;
Or place them on my hopeless heart:

But, shape or shade, whate'er thou art,   85
In mercy ne'er again depart!
Or farther with thee bear my soul
Than winds can waft or waters roll!

    . . . . .

    . . . . .

'Such is my name, and such my tale.
   Confessor, to thy secret ear   90
I breathe the sorrows I bewail,
   And thank thee for the generous tear
This glazing eye could never shed.
Then lay me with the humblest dead,
And, save the cross above my head,   95
Be neither name nor emblem spread,
By prying stranger to be read,
Or stay the passing pilgrim's tread.'

He passed – nor of his name and race
Hath left a token or a trace,   100
Save what the Father must not say
Who shrived him on his dying day:
This broken tale was all we knew
Of her he loved, or him he slew.

from The Bride of Abydos: A Turkish Tale

CANTO 2

22

Zuleika, mute and motionless,
Stood like that statue of distress,
When, her last hope for ever gone,
The mother hardened into stone:
All in the maid that eye could see   5
Was but a younger Niobé.
But ere her lip, or even her eye,

Essayed to speak, or look reply,
Beneath the garden's wicket porch
Far flashed on high a blazing torch!   10
Another – and another – and another –
'Oh fly – no more – yet now my more than brother!'
Far, wide, through every thicket spread,
The fearful lights are gleaming red;
Nor these alone – for each right hand   15
Is ready with a sheathless brand.
They part, pursue, return, and wheel
With searching flambeau, shining steel;
And last of all, his sabre waving,
Stern Giaffir in his fury raving: 20
And now almost they touch the cave –
Oh! must that grot be Selim's grave?

23

Dauntless he stood – ''Tis come – soon past –
One kiss, Zuleika – 'tis my last:
   But yet my band not far from shore   25
May hear this signal, see the flash;
Yet now too few – the attempt were rash:
   No matter – yet one effort more.'
Forth to the cavern mouth he stepped –
   His pistol's echo rang on high;   30
Zuleika started not, nor wept,
   Despair benumbed her breast and eye!
'They hear me not, or if they ply
Their oars, 'tis but to see me die;
That sound hath drawn my foes more nigh.   35
Then forth my father's scimitar,
Thou ne'er hast seen less equal war!
Farewell, Zuleika! – sweet! retire:
   Yet stay within – here linger safe,
   At thee his rage will only chafe.   40
Stir not – lest even to thee perchance
Some erring blade or ball should glance.
Fearest thou for him? – may I expire
If in this strife I seek thy sire!
No – though by him that poison poured;   45

No – though again he call me coward!
But tamely shall I meet their steel?
No – as each crest save *his* may feel!'

27

By Helle's stream there is a voice of wail!
And woman's eye is wet – man's cheek is pale: 50
Zuleika! last of Giaffir's race,
      Thy destined lord is come too late:
He sees not – ne'er shall see thy face!
              Can he not hear
The loud wul-wulleh warn his distant ear?   55
      Thy handmaids weeping at the gate,
      The Koran-chanters of the hymn of fate,
      The silent slaves with folded arms that wait,
Sighs in the hall, and shrieks upon the gale,
              Tell him thy tale!   60
Thou didst not view thy Selim fall!
      That fearful moment when he left the cave
              Thy heart grew chill:
He was thy hope – thy joy – thy love – thine all,
And that last thought on him thou couldst not save   65
              Sufficed to kill;
Burst forth in one loud cry – and all was still.
      Peace to thy broken heart, and virgin grave!
Ah! happy! but of life to lose the worst!
That grief – though deep – though fatal – was thy first!   70
Thrice happy ne'er to feel nor fear the force
Of absence, shame, pride, hate, revenge, remorse!
And, oh! that pang where more than madness lies!
The worm that will not sleep – and never dies;
Thought of the gloomy day and ghastly night,   75
That dreads the darkness, and yet loathes the light,
That winds around, and tears the quivering heart!
Ah! wherefore not consume it – and depart!
Woe to thee, rash and unrelenting chief!
      Vainly thou heapest the dust upon thy head,   80
      Vainly the sackcloth o'er thy limbs dost spread:

By that same hand, Abdallah, Selim bled,
Now let it tear thy beard in idle grief:
Thy pride of heart, thy bride for Osman's bed,
She, whom thy sultan had but seen to wed,   85
        Thy daughter's dead!
    Hope of thine age, thy twilight's lonely beam,
    The star hath set that shone on Helle's stream.
What quenched its ray? – the blood that thou hast shed!
Hark: to the hurried question of Despair,   90
'Where is my child?,' Echo answers – 'Where?'

                        28
Within the place of thousand tombs
    That shine beneath, while dark above
The sad but living cypress glooms
    And withers not, though branch and leaf   95
Are stamped with an eternal grief,
    Like early unrequited love,
One spot exists, which ever blooms,
    Even in that deadly grove –
A single rose is shedding there   100
    Its lonely lustre, meek and pale:
It looks as planted by Despair –
    So white – so faint – the slightest gale
Might whirl the leaves on high;
    And yet, though storms and blight assail,   105
And hands more rude than wintry sky
    May wring it from the stem – in vain –
    Tomorrow sees it bloom again:
The stalk some spirit gently rears,
And waters with celestial tears . . .   110

from The Corsair: A Tale

CANTO THE FIRST

1

'O'er the glad waters of the dark blue sea,
Our thoughts as boundless, and our souls as free,
Far as the breeze can bear, the billows foam,
Survey our empire, and behold our home!
These are our realms, no limits to their sway –   5
Our flag the sceptre all who meet obey.
Ours the wild life in tumult still to range
From toil to rest, and joy in every change.
Oh, who can tell? not thou, luxurious slave,
Whose soul would sicken o'er the heaving wave;   10
Not thou, vain lord of wantonness and ease,
Whom slumber soothes not, pleasure cannot please.
Oh, who can tell, save he whose heart hath tried,
And danced in triumph o'er the waters wide,
The exulting sense – the pulse's maddening play,   15
That thrills the wanderer of that trackless way?
That for itself can woo the approaching fight,
And turn what some deem danger to delight;
That seeks what cravens shun with more than zeal,
And where the feeble faint can only feel –   20
Feel – to the rising bosom's inmost core,
Its hope awaken and its spirit soar?
No dread of death if with us die our foes –
Save that it seems even duller than repose:
Come when it will – we snatch the life of life –   25
When lost – what recks it by disease or strife?
Let him who crawls enamoured of decay,
Cling to his couch, and sicken years away:
Heave his thick breath, and shake his palsied head;
Ours – the fresh turf, and not the feverish bed.   30
While gasp by gasp he falters forth his soul,
Ours with one pang – one bound – escapes control.
His corse may boast its urn and narrow cave,
And they who loathed his life may gild his grave:

Ours are the tears, though few, sincerely shed,   35
When Ocean shrouds and sepulchres our dead.
For us, even banquets fond regret supply
In the red cup that crowns our memory;
And the brief epitaph in danger's day,
When those who win at length divide the prey,   40
And cry, Remembrance saddening o'er each brow,
How had the brave who fell exulted *now*!'

                    2
Such were the notes that from the Pirate's isle
Around the kindling watch-fire rang the while . . .

THOMAS CAMPBELL

from The Pleasures of Hope

    Cease, every joy, to glimmer on my mind,
But leave – oh, leave the light of Hope behind!
What though my winged hours of bliss have been,
Like angel-visits, few and far between;
Her musing mood should every pang appease,   5
And charm, when pleasures lose the power to please!
Yes; let each rapture, dear to Nature, flee:
Close not the light of Fortune's stormy sea –
Mirth, Music, Friendship, Love's propitious smile,
Chase every care, and charm a little while,   10
Ecstatic throbs the fluttering heart employ,
And all her strings are harmonised to joy! –
But why so short is Love's delighted hour?
Why fades the dew on Beauty's sweetest flower?
Why can no hymned charm of music heal   15
The sleepless woes impassioned spirits feel?
Can Fancy's fairy hands no veil create
To hide the sad realities of Fate? –
    No! not the quaint remark, the sapient rule,

Nor all the pride of Wisdom's wordly school,   20
Have power to soothe, unaided and alone,
The heart that vibrates to a feeling tone!
When stepdame Nature every bliss recalls,
Fleet as the meteor o'er thc desert falls;
When, 'reft of all, yon widowed sire appears   25
A lonely hermit in the vale of years;
Say, can the world one joyous thought bestow
To Friendship, weeping at the couch of Woe?
No! but a brighter soothes the last adieu –
Souls of impassioned mould, she speaks to you!   30
Weep not, she says, at Nature's transient pain,
Congenial spirits part to meet again!

WILLIAM COWPER

from Truth

    The path to bliss abounds with many a snare;
Learning is one, and wit, however rare.
The Frenchman, first in literary fame,
(Mention him, if you please. Voltaire? – The same.)
With spirit, genius, eloquence, supplied,   5
Lived long, wrote much, laughed heartily, and died.
The scripture was his jest-book, whence he drew
Bon mots to gall the Christian and the Jew.
An infidel in health, but what when sick?
Oh – then a text would touch him at the quick.   10
View him at Paris, in his last career:
Surrounding throngs the demi-god revere;
Exalted on his pedestal of pride,
And fumed with frankincense on every side,
He begs their flattery with his latest breath;   15
And, smothered in it at last, is praised to death!
    Yon cottager, who weaves at her own door,

Pillow and bobbins all her little store;
Content, though mean; and cheerful, if not gay;
Shuffling her threads about the live-long day,   20
Just earns a scanty pittance; and at night
Lies down secure, her heart and pocket light:
She, for her humble sphere by nature fit,
Has little understanding, and no wit;
Receives no praise; but though her lot be such –   25
Toilsome and indigent – she renders much;
Just knows, and knows no more, her Bible true –
A truth the brilliant Frenchman never knew;
And in that charter reads, with sparkling eyes,
Her title to the treasure in the skies.   30
    Oh, happy peasant! Oh, unhappy bard!
His the mere tinsel, hers the rich reward;
He praised, perhaps, for ages yet to come;
She never heard of half a mile from home;
He, lost in errors, his vain heart prefers;   35
She, safe in the simplicity of hers.
    Not many wise, rich, noble or profound
In science, win one inch of heavenly ground.
And is it not a mortifying thought
The poor should gain it, and the rich should not?   40
No – the voluptuaries, who ne'er forget
One pleasure lost, lose heaven without regret;
Regret would rouse them, and give birth to prayer;
Prayer would add faith, and faith would fix them there.

Verses Supposed to be Written by Alexander Selkirk, during his solitary abode in the Island of Juan Fernandez

I am monarch of all I survey,
   My right there is none to dispute;
From the centre all round to the sea,
   I am lord of the fowl and the brute.
O Solitude! where are the charms   5
   That sages have seen in thy face?
Better dwell in the midst of alarms,
   Than reign in this horrible place.

I am out of humanity's reach,
   I must finish my journey alone,   10
Never hear the sweet music of speech –
   I start at the sound of my own.
The beasts that roam over the plain
   My form with indifference see;
They are so unacquainted with man,   15
   Their tameness is shocking to me.

Society, friendship, and love,
   Divinely bestowed upon man,
Oh, had I the wings of a dove,
   How soon would I taste you again!   20
My sorrows I then might assuage
   In the ways of religion and truth,
Might learn from the wisdom of age,
   And be cheered by the sallies of youth.

Religion! what treasure untold   25
   Resides in that heavenly word!
More precious than silver and gold,
   Or all that this earth can afford.

But the sound of the church-going bell
   These valleys and rocks never heard,   30
Ne'er sighed at the sound of a knell,
   Or smiled when a sabbath appeared.

Ye winds, that have made me your sport,
   Convey to this desolate shore
Some cordial endearing report   35
   Of a land I shall visit no more.
My friends, do they now and then send
   A wish or a thought after me?
O tell me I yet have a friend,
   Though a friend I am never to see.   40

How fleet is a glance of the mind!
   Compared with the speed of its flight,
The tempest itself lags behind,
   And the swift-winged arrows of light.
When I think of my own native land,   45
   In a moment I seem to be there;
But alas! recollection at hand
   Soon hurries me back to despair.

But the sea-fowl is gone to her nest,
   The beast is laid down in his lair,   50
Even here is a season of rest,
   And I to my cabin repair.
There is mercy in every place;
   And mercy, encouraging thought!
Gives even affliction a grace,   55
   And reconciles man to his lot.

Epitaph on a Hare

Here lies, whom hounds did ne'er pursue,
    Nor swifter greyhound follow,
Whose foot ne'er tainted morning dew,
    Nor ear heard huntsman's hallo'.

Old Tiney, surliest of his kind,   5
    Who, nursed with tender care,
And to domestic bounds confined,
    Was still a wild jack-hare.

Though duly from my hand he took
    His pittance every night,   10
He did it with a jealous look,
    And, when he could, would bite.

His diet was of wheaten bread,
    And milk, and oats, and straw,
Thistles, or lettuces instead,   15
    With sand to scour his maw.

On twigs of hawthorn he regaled,
    On pippins' russet peel;
And, when his juicy salads failed,
    Sliced carrot pleased him well.   20

A Turkey carpet was his lawn,
    Whereon he loved to bound,
To skip and gambol like a fawn,
    And swing his rump around.

His frisking was at evening hours,   25
    For then he lost his fear;
But most before approaching showers,
    Or when a storm drew near.

Eight years and five round-rolling moons
    He thus saw steal away,   30

Dozing out all his idle noons,
   And every night at play.

I kept him for his humour's sake,
   For he would oft beguile
My heart of thoughts that made it ache,   35
   And force me to a smile.

But now, beneath this walnut shade,
   He finds his long, last home,
And waits, in snug concealment laid,
   Till gentler puss shall come: 40

He, still more aged, feels the shocks
   From which no care can save,
And, partner once of Tiney's box,
   Must soon partake his grave.

The Task
from Book I, The Sofa

No tree in all the grove but has its charms,
Though each its hue peculiar; paler some,
And of a wannish grey: the willow such,
And poplar, that with silver lines his leaf,
And ash far-stretching his umbrageous arm;   5
Of deeper green the elm; and deeper still,
Lord of the woods, the long-surviving oak.
Some glossy-leaved, and shining in the sun,
The maple, and the beech of oily nuts
Prolific, and the lime at dewy eve   10
Diffusing odours: nor unnoted pass
The sycamore, capricious in attire,
Now green, now tawny, and, ere autumn yet
Have changed the woods, in scarlet honours bright.

O'er these, but far beyond (a spacious map   15
Of hill and valley interposed between),
The Ouse, dividing the well-watered land,
Now glitters in the sun, and now retires,
As bashful, yet impatient to be seen.
    Hence the declivity is sharp and short,   20
And such the re-ascent; between them weeps
A little naiad her impoverished urn
All summer long, which winter fills again.
The folded gates would bar my progress now,
But that the lord of this enclosed demesne,   25
Communicative of the good he owns,
Admits me to a share; the guiltless eye
Commits no wrong, nor wastes what it enjoys.
Refreshing change! Where now the blazing sun?
By short transition we have lost his glare,   30
And stepped at once into a cooler clime.
Ye fallen avenues! once more I mourn
Your fate unmerited, once more rejoice
That yet a remnant of your race survives.
How airy and how light the graceful arch,   35
Yet awful as the consecrated roof
Re-echoing pious anthems! while beneath
The chequered earth seems restless as a flood
Brushed by the wind. So sportive is the light
Shot through the boughs, it dances as they dance,   40
Shadow and sunshine intermingling quick,
And darkening and enlightening, as the leaves
Play wanton, every moment, every spot.
    And now, with nerves new-braced and spirits cheered,
We tread the wilderness, whose well-rolled walks,   45
With curvature of slow and easy sweep –
Deception innocent – give ample space
To narrow bounds . . .

from Book IV, The Winter Evening

Just when our drawing rooms begin to blaze
With lights, by clear reflection multiplied
From many a mirror, in which he of Gath,
Goliath, might have seen his giant bulk
Whole, without stooping, towering crest and all,   5
My pleasures, too, begin. But me, perhaps,
The glowing hearth may satisfy awhile
With faint illumination, that uplifts
The shadow to the ceiling, there by fits
Dancing uncouthly to the quivering flame.   10
Not undelightful is an hour to me
So spent in parlour twilight: such a gloom
Suits well the thoughtful or unthinking mind,
The mind contemplative, with some new theme
Pregnant, or indisposed alike to all.   15
Laugh ye, who boast your more mercurial powers,
That never feel a stupor, know no pause,
Nor need one; I am conscious, and confess,
Fearless, a soul that does not always think.
Me oft has fancy, ludicrous and wild,   20
Soothed with a waking dream of houses, towers,
Trees, churches, and strange visages, expressed
In the red cinders, while with poring eye
I gazed, myself creating what I saw.
Nor less amused have I quiescent watched   25
The sooty films that play upon the bars,
Pendulous, and foreboding, in the view
Of superstition, prophesying still,
Though still deceived, some stranger's near approach.
'Tis thus the understanding takes repose   30
In indolent vacuity of thought,
And sleeps and is refreshed.

from Book VI, The Winter Walk at Noon

But let the months go round, a few short months,
And all shall be restored. These naked shoots,
Barren as lances, among which the wind
Makes wintry music, sighing as it goes,
Shall put their graceful foliage on again, 5
And, more aspiring, and with ampler spread,
Shall boast new charms, and more than they have lost.
Then, each in its peculiar honours clad,
Shall publish, even to the distant eye,
Its family and tribe. Laburnum, rich 10
In streaming gold; syringa, ivory pure;
The scentless and the scented rose: this red
And of an humbler growth, the other tall,
And throwing up into the darkest gloom
Of neighbouring cypress, or more sable yew, 15
Her silver globes, light as the foamy surf
That the wind severs from the broken wave . . .

from Tirocinium: or, A Review of Schools

Oh 'tis a sight to be with joy perused,
By all whom sentiment has not abused;
(New-fangled sentiment, the boasted grace
Of those who never feel in the right place);
A sight surpassed by none that we can show, 5
Though Vestris on one leg still shine below:
A father blest with an ingenuous son –
Father, and friend, and tutor, all in one.
How! – turn again to tales long since forgot,

Aesop, and Phaedrus, and the rest? – Why not?   10
He will not blush that has his father's heart,
To take in childish plays a childish part;
But bends his sturdy back to any toy
That youth takes pleasure in, to please his boy:
Then why resign into a stranger's hand   15
A task as much within your own command,
That God and nature, and your interest too,
Seem with one voice to delegate to you?
Why hire a lodging in a house unknown
For one whose tenderest thoughts all hover round your own?   20
This second weaning, needless as it is,
How does it lacerate both your heart and his!
The indented stick, that loses day by day
Notch after notch, till all are smoothed away,
Bears witness, long ere his dismission come,   25
With what intense desire he wants his home.
But, though the joys he hopes beneath your roof
Bid fair enough to answer in the proof,
Harmless, and safe, and natural, as they are,
A disappointment waits him even there: 30
Arrived, he feels an unexpected change;
He blushes, hangs his head, is shy and strange,
No longer takes, as once with fearless ease,
His favourite stand between his father's knees,
But seeks the corner of some distant seat,   35
And eyes the door, and watches a retreat,
And, least familiar where he should be most,
Feels all his happiest privileges lost.
Alas, poor boy! – the natural effect
Of love by absence chilled into respect.   40

GEORGE CRABBE

Tales, 1812
from Tale 3, The Gentleman Farmer

Two are the species in this genus known:
One, who is rich in his profession grown,
Who yearly finds his ample stores increase
From fortune's favours and a favouring lease;
Who rides his hunter, who his house adorns;   5
Who drinks his wine, and his disbursement scorns;
Who freely lives, and loves to show he can –
This is the farmer made the gentleman.
    The second species from the world is sent,
Tired with its strife, or with his wealth content;   10
In books and men beyond the former read,
To farming solely by a passion led,
Or by a fashion; curious in his land;
Now planning much, now changing what he planned;
Pleased by each trial, not by failures vexed,   15
And ever certain to succeed the next;
Quick to resolve, and easy to persuade –
This is the gentleman a farmer made.
    Gwyn was one of these; he from the world withdrew
Early in life, his reasons known to few;   20
Some disappointment said, some pure good sense,
The love of the land, the press of indolence;
His fortune known, and coming to retire,
If not a farmer, men had called him squire.
    Forty and five his years, no child or wife   25
Crossed the still tenor of his chosen life;
Much land he purchased, planted far around,
And let some portions of superfluous ground
To farmers near him: not displeased to say,
'My tenants,' nor 'our worthy landlord,' they.   30
    Fixed in his farm, he soon displayed his skill
In small-boned lambs, the horse-hoe, and the drill;
From these he rose to themes of nobler kind,

And showed the riches of a fertile mind;
To all around their visits he repaid,   35
And thus his mansion and himself displayed.
His rooms were stately, rather fine than neat,
And guests politely called his house a seat;
At much expense was each apartment graced,
His taste was gorgeous, but it still was taste;   40
In full festoons the crimson curtains fell,
The sofas rose in bold elastic swell . . .

from Tale 11, Edward Shore

Genius! thou gift of heaven! thou light divine!
Amid what dangers art thou doomed to shine!
Oft will the body's weakness check thy force,
Oft damp thy vigour, and impede thy course;
And trembling nerves compel thee to restrain   5
Thy nobler efforts, to contend with pain;
Or Want (sad guest!) will in thy presence come,
And breath around her melancholy gloom;
To life's low cares will thy proud thought confine,
And make her sufferings, her impatience, thine.   10
       Evil and strong, seducing passions prey
On soaring minds, and win them from their way,
Who then to vice the subject spirits give,
And in the service of the conqueror live:
Like captive Samson making sport for all,   15
Who feared their strength, and glory in their fall.
       Genius, with virtue, still may lack the aid
Implored by humble minds and hearts afraid;
May leave to timid souls the shield and sword
Of the tried faith, and the resistless word;   20
Amid a world of dangers venturing forth,
Frail, but yet fearless, proud in conscious worth,
Till strong temptation, in some fatal time,
Assails the heart, and wins the soul to crime;

When left by honour, and by sorrow spent, 25
Unused to pray, unable to repent,
The nobler powers that once exalted high
The aspiring man, shall then degraded lie:
Reason, through anguish, shall her throne forsake,
And strength of mind but stronger madness make. 30

    When Edward Shore had reached his twentieth year,
He felt his bosom light, his conscience clear;
Applause at school the youthful hero gained,
And trials there with manly strength sustained:
With prospects bright upon the world he came, 35
Pure love of virtue, strong desire of fame:
Men watched the way his lofty mind would take,
And all foretold the progress he would make.

    Boast of these friends, to older men a guide,
Proud of his parts, but gracious in his pride; 40
He bore a gay good-nature in his face,
And in his air were dignity and grace;
Dress that became his state and years he wore,
And sense and spirit shone in Edward Shore.

    Thus, while admiring friends the youth beheld, 45
His own disgust their forward hopes repelled;
For he unfixed, unfixing, looked around,
And no employment but in seeking found;
He gave his restless thoughts to views refined,
And shrank from worldly cares with wounded mind. 50

    Rejecting trade, awhile he dwelt on laws,
'But who could plead, if unapproved the cause?'
A doubting, dismal tribe physicians seemed;
Divines o'er texts and disputations dreamed;
War and its glory he perhaps could love, 55
But there again, he must the cause approve.

    Our hero thought no deed should gain applause
Where timid virtue found support in laws;
He to all good would soar, would fly all sin,
By the pure prompting of the will within; 60
'Who needs a law that binds him not to steal,'
Asked the young teacher, 'can he rightly feel?
To curb the will, or arm in honour's cause,

Or aid the weak – are these enforced by laws?
Should we a foul, ungenerous action dread,   65
Because a law condemns the adulterous bed?
Or fly pollution, not for fear of stain,
But that some statute tells us to refrain?
The grosser herd in ties like these we bind:
In virtue's freedom moves the enlightened mind.'   70

DAVID GARRICK

A Riddle

Kitty, a fair but frozen maid,
    Kindled a flame I still deplore;
The hood-winked boy I called in aid,
Much of his near approach afraid,
    So fatal to my suit before.   5

At length, propitious to my prayer,
    The little urchin came;
At once he sought the midway air,
And soon he cleared, with dextrous care,
    The bitter relics of my flame.   10

To Kitty, Fanny now succeeds:
    She kindles slow, but lasting, fires:
With care my appetite she feeds;
Each day some willing victim bleeds
    To satisfy my strange desires.   15

Say, by what title, or what name,
    Must I this youth address?
Cupid and he are not the same,
Though both can raise, or quench, a flame –
    I'll kiss you, if you guess.   20

JOHN GAY

The Hare and Many Friends

Friendship, like love, is but a name
Unless to one you stint the flame.
The child whom many fathers share
Hath seldom known a father's care;
'Tis thus in friendships: who depend   5
On many, rarely find a friend.

   A hare, who in a civil way,
Complied with everything, like Gay,
Was known by all the bestial train
Who haunt the wood or graze the plain: 10
Her care was never to offend,
And every creature was her friend.
   As forth she went at early dawn
To taste the dew-besprinkled lawn,
Behind she hears the hunter's cries,   15
And from the deep-mouthed thunder flies;
She starts, she stops, she pants for breath,
She hears the near advance of death;
She doubles, to mislead the hound,
And measures back her mazy round   20
Till, fainting in the public way,
Half-dead with fear she gasping lay.
   What transport in her bosom grew,
When first the horse appeared in view!
'Let me,' says she, 'your back ascend,   25
And owe my safety to a friend;
You know my feet betray my flight:
To friendship every burden's light.'
   The horse replied, 'Poor honest puss,
It grieves my heart to see thee thus: 30
Be comforted, relief is near,
For all your friends are in the rear.'
   She next the stately bull implored,

And thus replied the mighty lord:
'Since every beast alive can tell   35
That I sincerely wish you well,
I may, without offence, pretend
To take the freedom of a friend:
Love calls me hence – a favourite cow
Expects me near yon barley mow;   40
And when a lady's in the case,
You know, all other things give place.
To leave you thus might seem unkind;
But see, the goat is just behind.'

    The goat remarked her pulse was high,   45
Her languid head, her heavy eye:
'My back,' she said, 'may do you harm;
The sheep's at hand, and wool is warm.'

    The sheep was feeble, and complained
His sides a load of wool sustained;   50
Said he was slow, confessed his fears,
For hounds eat sheep as well as hares.

    She now the trotting calf addressed,
To save from death a friend distressed.

    'Shall I,' says she, 'of tender age   55
In this important care engage?
Older and abler passed you by;
How strong are those! How weak am I!
Should I presume to bear you hence,
Those friends of mine may take offence.   60
Excuse me, then. You know my heart.
But dearest friends, alas, must part.
How shall we all lament! Adieu.
For see, the hounds are just in view.'

OLIVER GOLDSMITH

'When Lovely Woman Stoops to Folly'

When lovely woman stoops to folly,
    And finds too late that men betray,
What charm can soothe her melancholy,
    What art can wash her guilt away?

The only art her guilt to cover,   5
    To hide her shame from every eye,
To give repentance to her lover,
    And wring his bosom – is, to die.

THOMAS GRAY

from Elegy Written in a Country Churchyard

The curfew tolls the knell of parting day,
The lowing herd wind slowly o'er the lea,
The ploughman homeward plods his weary way,
And leaves the world to darkness and to me.

Now fades the glimmering landscape on the sight,   5
And all the air a solemn stillness holds,
Save where the beetle wheels his droning flight,
And drowsy tinklings lull the distant folds;

Save that from yonder ivy-mantled tower
The moping owl does to the moon complain   10
Of such as, wandering near her secret bower,
Molest her ancient, solitary reign.

Beneath those rugged elms, that yew tree's shade,
Where heaves the turf in many a mouldering heap,

Each in his narrow cell for ever laid,   15
The rude forefathers of the hamlet sleep.

The breezy call of incense-breathing morn,
The swallow twittering from the straw-built shed,
The cock's shrill clarion or the echoing horn,
No more shall rouse them from their lowly bed.   20

For them no more the blazing hearth shall burn,
Or busy housewife ply her evening care:
No children run to lisp their sire's return,
Or climb his knees the envied kiss to share.

Oft did the harvest to their sickle yield,   25
Their furrow oft the stubborn glebe has broke;
How jocund did they drive their team afield!
How bowed the woods beneath their sturdy stroke!

Let not Ambition mock their useful toil,
Their homely joys and destiny obscure;   30
Nor Grandeur hear, with a disdainful smile,
The short and simple annals of the poor:

The boast of heraldry, the pomp of power,
And all that beauty, all that wealth e'er gave,
Awaits alike the inevitable hour.   35
The paths of glory lead but to the grave.

Nor you, ye proud, impute to these the fault
If Memory o'er their tombs no trophies raise
Where, through the long-drawn isle and fretted vault,
The pealing anthem swells the note of praise.   40

Can storied urn or animated bust
Back to its mansion call the fleeting breath?
Can Honour's voice provoke the silent dust,
Or Flattery soothe the dull, cold ear of Death?

Perhaps in this neglected spot is laid   45
Some heart once pregnant with celestial fire;
Hands that the rod of empire might have swayed,
Or waked to ecstasy the living lyre.

But Knowledge to their eyes her ample page
Rich with the spoils of time did ne'er unroll;   50
Chill Penury repressed their noble rage,
And froze the genial current of the soul.

Full many a gem of purest ray serene
The dark, unfathomed caves of ocean bear;
Full many a flower is born to blush unseen,   55
And waste its sweetness on the desert air.

Some village-Hampden that with dauntless breast
The little tyrant of his field withstood;
Some mute, inglorious Milton here may rest;
Some Cromwell guiltless of his country's blood.   60

The applause of listening senates to command,
The threats of pain and ruin to despise,
To scatter plenty o'er a smiling land,
And read their history in a nation's eyes,

Their lot forbade: nor circumscribed alone   65
Their growing virtues, but their crimes confined;
Forbade to wade through slaughter to a throne,
And shut the gates of mercy on mankind.'

JAMES MERRICK

The Chameleon: A Fable after Monsieur de la Motte

Oft has it been my lot to mark
A proud, conceited, talking spark,
With eyes that hardly served at most
To guard their master 'gainst a post;
Yet round the world the blade has been   5
To see whatever could be seen,
Returning from his finished tour
Grown ten times perter than before.
Whatever word you chance to drop,
The travelled fool your mouth will stop: 10
'Sir, if my judgement you'll allow –
I've seen – and, sure, I ought to know' –
So begs you'd pay a due submission,
And acquiesce in his decision.

    Two travellers of such a cast,   15
As o'er Arabia's wilds they passed,
And on their way in friendly chat
Now talked of this and then of that,
Discoursed awhile, 'mongst other matter,
Of the chameleon's form and nature.   20
'A stranger animal,' cries one,
'Sure never lived beneath the sun.
A lizard's body lean and long,
A fish's head, a serpent's tongue,
Its tooth with triple claw disjoined –   25
And what a length of tail behind!
How slow its pace: and then, its hue –
Whoever saw so fine a blue?'

    'Hold there,' the other quick replies,
''Tis green – I saw it with these eyes   30
As late with open mouth it lay,
And warmed it in the sunny ray.
Stretched at its ease the beast I viewed,

And saw it eat the air for food.'
   'I've seen it, sir, as well as you,   35
And must again affirm it blue:
At leisure I the beast surveyed
Extended in the cooling shade.'
   ''Tis green, 'tis green, sir, I assure ye –';
'Green!' cries the other in a fury –   40
'Why, sir, d'ye think I've lost my eyes?'
''Twere no great loss,' the friend replies,
'For if they always serve you thus,
You'll find them but of little use.'
   So high at last the contest rose,   45
From words they almost came to blows,
When luckily came by a third –
To him the question they referred,
And begged he'd tell them, if he knew,
Whether the thing was green or blue.   50
   'Sirs,' cries the umpire, 'cease your pother –
The creature's neither one nor t'other.
I caught the animal last night,
And viewed it o'er by candle light.
I marked it well, 'twas black as jet –   55
You stare – but, sirs, I've got it yet,
And can produce it.' 'Pray, sir, do:
I'll lay my life the thing is blue.'
'And I'll be sworn that when you've seen
The reptile, you'll pronounce him green.'   60
   'Well, then, at once to ease the doubt,'
Replies the man, 'I'll turn him out:
And when before your eyes I've set him,
If you don't find him black, I'll eat him.'
He said; then, full before their sight,   65
Produced the beast, and lo! 'twas white.
Both stared; the man looked wondrous wise –
   'My children,' the chameleon cries
(Then first the creature found a tongue),
'You all are right, and all are wrong: 70
When next you talk of what you view,
Think others see as well as you;
Nor wonder if you find that none
Prefers your eyesight to his own.'

JOHN MILTON

from L'Allegro

Thus done the tales, to bed they creep,
By whispering winds soon lulled asleep.
Towered cities please us then,
And the busy hum of men,
Where throngs of knights and barons bold   5
In weeds of peace high triumphs hold
With store of ladies, whose bright eyes
Rain influence, and judge the prize
Of wit or arms, while both contend
To win her grace whom all commend.   10
There let Hymen oft appear
In saffron robe, with taper clear,
And pomp, and feast, and revelry,
With masque, and antique pageantry –
Such sights as youthful poets dream   15
On summer eves by haunted stream.
Then to the well-trod stage anon,
If Jonson's learned sock be on,
Or sweetest Shakespeare, Fancy's child,
Warble his native wood-notes wild.   20
And ever, against eating cares,
Lap me in soft Lydian airs
Married to immortal verse,
Such as the meeting soul may pierce
In notes, with many a winding bout   25
Of linked sweetness long drawn out
With wanton heed and giddy cunning,
The melting voice through mazes running,
Untwisting all the chains that tie
The hidden soul of harmony: 30
That Orpheus' self may heave his head
From golden slumber on a bed
Of heaped Elysian flowers, and hear
Such strains as would have won the ear
Of Pluto, to have quite set free   35

His half-regained Eurydice.
These delights, if thou canst give,
Mirth, with thee I mean to live.

from **Paradise Lost, Book V**

Now Morn, her rosy steps in the eastern clime
Advancing, sowed the earth with orient pearl,
When Adam waked – so customed, for his sleep
Was airy light, from pure digestion bred
And temperate vapours bland, which the only sound   · 5
Of leaves and fuming rills, Aurora's fan,
Lightly dispersed, and the shrill matin song
Of birds on every bough. So much the more
His wonder was to find unwakened Eve
With tresses discomposed, and glowing cheek,   10
As through unquiet rest. He on his side
Leaning half-raised, with looks of cordial love
Hung over her, enamoured, and beheld
Beauty which, whether waking or asleep,
Shot forth peculiar graces. Then with voice   15
Mild, as when Zephyrus on Flora breathes,
Her hand soft touching, whispered thus: 'Awake,
My fairest, my espoused, my latest found,
Heaven's last best gift, my ever new delight!
Awake! The morning shines, and the fresh field   20
Calls us: we lose the prime, to mark how spring
Our tended plants, how blows the citron grove,
What drops the myrrh, and what the balmy reed,
How Nature paints her colours, how the bee
Sits on the bloom extracting liquid sweet.'   25
   Such whispering waked her, but with startled eye
On Adam, whom embracing, thus she spake:
   'O sole in whom my thoughts find all repose –
My glory, my perfection; glad I see

Thy face, and morn returned, for I this night   30
(Such night till this I never passed) have dreamed –
If dreamed – not as I oft am wont, of thee,
Works of day past, or morrow's next design,
But of offence and trouble, which my mind
Knew never till this irksome night. Methought   35
Close at mine ear one called me forth to walk
With gentle voice: I thought it thine. It said,
"Why sleepest thou, Eve? Now is the pleasant time,
The cool, the silent, save where silence yields
To the night-warbling bird that, now awake,   40
Tunes sweetest his love-laboured song. Now reigns
Full-orbed the moon and, with more pleasing light,
Shadowy sets off the face of things. In vain,
If none regard, heaven wakes with all his eyes,
Whom to behold but thee, Nature's desire,   45
In whose sight all things joy, with ravishment
Attracted by thy beauty still to gaze?"
I rose at thy call, but found thee not;
To find thee I directed then my walk,
And on, methought, alone I passed through ways   50
That brought me on a sudden to the tree
Of interdicted knowledge. Fair it seemed –
Much fairer to my fancy than by day;
And as I, wondering, looked, beside it stood
One shaped and winged like one of those from heaven   55
By us oft seen: his dewy locks distilled
Ambrosia. On that tree he also gazed,
And, "O fair plant," said he, "with fruit surcharged;
Deigns none to ease thy load and taste thy sweet,
Nor God nor man? Is knowledge so despised?   60
Or envy or what reserve forbids to taste?
Forbid who will, none shall from me withhold
Longer thy offered good, why else set here?"
This said, he paused not, but with venturous arm
He plucked, he tasted. Me damp horror chilled   65
At such bold words vouched with a deed so bold;
But he thus, overjoyed: "O fruit divine,
Sweet of thyself, but much more sweet thus cropped,

Forbidden here, it seems, as only fit
For gods, yet able to make gods of men: 70
And why not gods of men, since good, the more
Communicated, more abundant grows,
The author not impaired but honoured more?
Here, happy creature, fair angelic Eve,
Partake thou also . . ." '   75

THOMAS MOSS

The Beggar's Petition

Amidst the more important toils of state,
   The counsels labouring in this patriot soul,
Though Europe from thy voice expect her fate,
   And thy keen glance extend from pole to pole;

O Chatham, nursed in ancient virtue's lore,   5
   To these sad strains incline a favouring ear;
Think on the God whom thou, and I, adore,
   Nor turn unpitying from the poor man's prayer.

Pity the sorrows of a poor old man
   Whose trembling limbs have borne him to your door,   10
Whose days are dwindled to the shortest span –
   Oh, give relief, and heaven will bless your store.

Ah me! how blest was once a peasant's life!
   No lawless passion swelled my even breast;
Far from the stormy waves of civil strife   15
   Sound were my slumber, and my heart at rest.

I ne'er for guilty, painful pleasures roved,
   But, taught by nature, and by choice, to wed,
From all the hamlet culled whom best I loved:
   With her I stayed my heart, with her my bed.   20

To gild her worth I asked no wealthy power –
    My toil could feed her, and my arm defend;
In youth, or age, in pain, or pleasure's hour,
    The same fond husband, father, brother, friend.

And she, the faithful partner of my care,   25
    When ruddy evening streaked the western sky,
Looked towards the uplands, if her mate was there,
    Or through the beech wood cast an anxious eye;

Then, careful matron, heaped the ample board
    With savoury herbs, and picked the nicer part   30
From such plain food as Nature could afford,
    Ere simple Nature was debauched by Art.

While I, contented with my homely cheer,
    Saw round my knees my prattling childen play;
And oft with pleased attention sat to hear   35
    The little history of their idle day.

But ah! how changed the scene! On the cold stones,
    Where wont at night to blaze the cheerful fire,
Pale Famine sits and counts her naked bones,
    Still sighs for food, still pines with vain desire.   40

My faithful wife, with ever-straining eyes,
    Hangs on my bosom her dejected head;
My helpless infants raise their feeble cries,
    And from their father claim their daily bread.

Dear tender pledges of my honest love,   45
    On that bare bed behold your brother lie;
Three tedious days with pinching want he strove,
    The fourth, I saw the helpless cherub die.

Nor long shall ye remain. With visage sour
    Our tyrant lord commands us from our home   50
And, armed with cruel Law's coercive power,
    Bids me and mine o'er barren mountains roam.

Yet never, Chatham, have I passed a day
   In Riot's orgies, or in idle ease;
Ne'er have I sacrificed to sport and play,   55
   Or wished a pampered appetite to please.

Hard was my fate, and constant was my toil:
   Still with the morning's orient light I rose,
Felled the stout oak, or raised the lofty pile,
   Parched with the sun, in dark December froze.   60

Is it that Nature with a niggard hand
   Withholds her gifts from these once-favoured plains?
Has God, in vengeance to a guilty land,
   Sent Dearth and Famine to her labouring swains?

Ah no; yon hill, where daily sweats my brow,   65
   A thousand flocks, a thousand herds adorn;
Yon field, where late I drove the painful plough,
   Feels all her acres crowned with wavy corn.

But what avails that o'er the furrowed soil
   In Autumn's heat the yellow harvests rise,   70
If artificial want elude my toil,
   Untasted plenty wound my craving eyes?

What profits that at distance I behold
   My wealthy neighbour's fragrant smoke ascend,
If still the gripping cormorant withhold   75
   The fruits which rain and genial seasons send;

If those fell vipers of the public weal
   Yet unrelenting on our bowels prey;
If still the curse of penury we feel,
   And in the midst of plenty pine away;   80

In every port the vessel rides secure
   That wafts our harvest to a foreign shore,
While we the pangs of pressing want endure,
   The sons of strangers riot on our store?

O generous Chatham, stop those fatal sails,   85
    Once more with outstretched arm thy Britons save;
The unheeding crew but wait for favouring gales;
    O stop them ere they stem Italia's wave.

From thee alone I hope for instant aid,
    'Tis thou alone canst save my children's breath: 90
O deem not little of our cruel meed,
    O haste to help us, for delay is death.

So may nor Spleen nor Envy blast thy name,
    Nor voice profane thy patriot acts deride;
Still mayest thou stand the first in honest fame,   95
    Unstung by Folly, Vanity, or Pride.

So may thy languid limbs with strength be braced,
    And glowing health support thy active soul,
With fair renown thy public virtue graced,
    Far as thou badest Britannia's thunders roll.   100

Then joy to thee, and to thy children peace,
    The grateful hind shall drink from Plenty's horn:
And while they share the cultured land's increase,
    The poor shall bless the day when Pitt was born.

ALEXANDER POPE

from An Essay on Criticism

A little learning is a dangerous thing;
Drink deep, or taste not the Pierian spring:
There shallow draughts intoxicate the brain,
And drinking largely sobers us again.
Fired at first sight with what the Muse imparts,   5
In fearless youth we tempt the height of arts,
While from the bounded level of our mind

Short views we take, nor see the lengths behind,
But, more advanced, behold with strange surprise
New, distant, scenes of endless science rise!   10
So, pleased at first, the towering Alps we try,
Mount o'er the vales, and seem to tread the sky:
The eternal snows appear already past,
And the first clouds and mountains seem the last;
But, those attained, we tremble to survey   15
The growing labours of the lengthened way:
The increasing prospect tires our wandering eyes,
Hills peep o'er hills, and Alps on Alps arise!

Elegy to the Memory of an Unfortunate Lady

What beckoning ghost along the moonlit shade
Invites my step, and points to yonder glade?
'Tis she! – but why that bleeding bosom gored,
Why dimly gleams the visionary sword?
O, ever beauteous, ever friendly: tell,   5
Is it, in heaven, a crime to love too well?
To bear too tender or too firm a heart?
To act a lover's or a Roman's part?
Is there no bright reversion in the sky
For those who greatly think, or bravely die?   10
    Why bade ye else, ye powers, her soul aspire
Above the vulgar flight of low desire?
Ambition first sprung from your blest abodes,
The glorious fault of angels and of gods:
Thence to their images on earth it flows,   15
And in the breasts of kings and heroes glows.
Most souls, 'tis true, but peep out once an age,
Dull, sullen prisoners in the body's cage:
Dim lights of life that burn a length of years,
Useless, unseen, as lamps in sepulchres;   20
Like eastern kings a lazy state they keep,
And close confined to their own palace sleep.

From these, perhaps, ere Nature bade her die,
Fate snatched her early to the pitying sky.
As into air the purer spirits flow,   25
And separate from their kindred dregs below,
So flew the soul to its congenial place,
Nor left one virtue to redeem her race.
But thou, false guardian of a charge too good,
Thou, mean deserter of thy brother's blood,   30
See on these ruby lips the trembling breath,
These cheeks, now fading at the blast of death:
Cold is that breast which warmed the world before,
And those love-darting eyes must roll no more.
Thus, if eternal justice rules the ball,   35
Thus shall your wives, and thus your children fall:
On all the line a sudden vengeance waits,
And frequent hearses shall besiege your gates.
There passengers shall stand, and pointing say
(While the long funerals blacken all the way),   40
'Lo, these were they whose souls the Furies steeled,
And cursed with hearts unknowing how to yield.
Thus, unlamented, pass the proud away,
The gaze of fools and pageant of a day!
So perish all whose breast ne'er learned to glow   45
For others' good, or melt at others' woe.'
What can atone, O ever-injured shade,
Thy fate unpitied, and thy rites unpaid?
No friend's complaint, no kind domestic tear
Pleased thy pale ghost, or graced thy mournful bier.   50
By foreign hands thy dying eyes were closed,
By foreign hands thy decent limbs composed,
By foreign hands thy humble grave adorned,
By strangers honoured, and by strangers mourned.
What though no friends in sable weeds appear,   55
Grieve for an hour, perhaps, then mourn a year,
And bear about the mockery of woe
To midnight dances and the public show?
What though no weeping Loves thy ashes grace,
Nor polished marble emulate thy face?   60
What though no sacred earth allow thee room,
Nor hallowed dirge be muttered o'er thy tomb?

Yet shall thy grave with rising flowers be dressed,
And the green turf lie lightly on thy breast:
There shall the morn her earliest tears bestow,   65
There the first roses of the year shall blow,
While angels with their silvery wings o'ershade
The ground, now sacred by thy relics made.
    So, peaceful, rests, without a stone, a name,
What once had beauty, titles, wealth and fame.   70
How loved, how honoured once, avails thee not,
To whom related, or by whom begot;
A heap of dust alone remains of thee:
'Tis all thou art, and all the proud shall be.
    Poets themselves must fall, like those they sung;   75
Deaf the praised ear, and mute the tuneful tongue.
Even he, whose soul now melts in mournful lays,
Shall shortly want the generous tear he pays;
Then from his closing eyes thy form shall part,
And the last pang shall tear thee from his heart,   80
Life's idle business at one gasp be o'er,
The Muse forgot, and thou beloved no more.

from An Essay on Man, Epistle I

    What if the foot, ordained the dust to tread,
Or hand to toil, aspired to be the head?
What if the head, the eye, or ear, repined
To serve mere engines to the ruling mind?
Just as absurd for any part to claim   5
To be another, in this general frame:
Just as absurd, to mourn the tasks or pains
The great directing Mind of All ordains.
    All are but parts of one stupendous whole,
Whose body, Nature is, and God the soul;   10
That, changed through all, and yet in all the same,
Great in the earth as in the ethereal frame,
Warms in the sun, refreshes in the breeze,

Glows in the stars, and blossoms in the trees,
Lives through all life, extends through all extent,   15
Spreads undivided, operates unspent,
Breathes in our soul, informs our mortal part,
As full, as perfect, in a hair as heart;
As full, as perfect, in vile man that mourns
As the rapt seraph that adores and burns;   20
To him no high, no low, no great, no small:
He fills, he bounds, connects, and equals all.
     Cease, then nor Order imperfection name:
Our proper bliss depends on what we blame.
Know thy own point: this kind, this due degree   25
Of blindness, weakness, heaven bestows on thee.
Submit – in this, or any other, sphere,
Secure to be as blest as thou canst bear;
Safe in the hand of one disposing power,
Or in the natal, or the mortal hour.   30
All nature is but art, unknown to thee;
All chance, direction which thou canst not see;
All discord, harmony not understood;
All partial evil, universal good:
And, spite of pride, in erring reason's spite,   35
One truth is clear: Whatever is, is right.

MATTHEW PRIOR

from Henry and Emma: A Poem, upon the Model of the Nut-Brown Maid

Emma
With fatal certainty Thalestris knew
To send the arrow from the twanging yew;
And, great in arms and foremost in the war,
Bonduca brandished high the British spear.
Could thirst of vengeance and desire of fame   5

Excite the female breast with martial flame?
And shall not love's diviner power inspire
More hardy virtue and more generous fire?
    Near thee, mistrust not, constant I'll abide,
And fall, or vanquish, fighting by thy side.   10
Though my inferior strength may not allow
That I should bear or draw the warrior bow,
With ready hand I will the shaft supply,
And joy to see thy victor arrows fly.
Touched in the battle by the hostile reed   15
Should'st thou (but heaven avert it!) should'st thou bleed,
To stop the wounds my finest lawn I'd tear,
Wash them with tears, and wipe them with my hair:
Blest, when my dangers and my toils have shown
That I, of all mankind, could love but thee alone.   20

                    Henry
    But canst thou, tender maid, canst thou sustain
Afflictive want, or hunger's pressing pain?
Those limbs, in lawn and softest silk arrayed,
From sunbeams guarded, and of winds afraid,
Can they bear angry Jove? Can they resist   25
The parching Dog-star and the bleak north east?
When chilled by adverse snows and beating rain
We tread with weary steps the longsome plain;
When with hard toil we seek our evening food,
Berries and acorns, from the neighbouring wood,   30
And find among the cliffs no other house
But the thin covert of some gathered boughs;
Wilt thou not then reluctant send thine eye
Around the dreary waste and, weeping, try
(Though then, alas, that trial be too late)   35
To find thy father's hospitable gate
And seats, where Ease and Plenty brooding sat –
Those seats, whence long excluded, thou must mourn;
That gate, forever barred to thy return?
Wilt thou not then bewail ill-fated love,   40
And hate a banished man condemned in woods to rove?

                    Emma
    Thy rise of fortune did I only wed,

From its decline determined to recede?
Did I but purpose to embark with thee
On the smooth surface of a summer's sea,   45
While gentle zephyrs play in prosperous gales,
And Fortune's favour fills the swelling sails,
But would forsake the ship, and make the shore,
When the winds whistle and the tempests roar?
No, Henry, no: one sacred oath has tied   50
Our loves, one destiny our life shall guide,
Nor wild nor deep our common way divide.
   When from the cave thou risest with the day
To beat the woods and rouse the bounding prey,
The cave with moss and branches I'll adorn,   55
And cheerful sit, to wait my lord's return.
And when thou frequent bring'st the smitten deer
(For seldom, archers say, thy arrows err),
I'll fetch quick fuel from the neighbouring wood,
And strike the sparkling flint, and dress the food: 60
With humble duty and officious haste
I'll cull the furthest mead for thy repast;
The choicest herbs I to thy board will bring,
And draw thy water from the freshest spring;
And when, at night, with weary toil oppressed,   65
Soft slumbers thou enjoyest, and wholesome rest,
Watchful I'll guard thee, and with midnight prayer
Weary the gods to keep thee in their care,
And joyous ask, at morn's returning ray,
If thou hast health, and I may bless the day.   70
My thoughts shall fix, my latest wish depend,
On thee, guide, guardian, kinsman, father, friend:
By all these sacred names be Henry known
To Emma's heart, and grateful let him own
That she, of all mankind, could love but him alone.   75

Henry
   Vainly thou tellest me what the woman's care
Shall in the wildness of the wood prepare:
Thou, e'er thou goest, unhappiest of thy kind,
Must leave the habit and the sex behind.

No longer shall thy comely tresses break 80
In flowing ringlets on thy snowy neck,
Or sit behind thy head, an ample round,
In graceful braids with various ribbon bound:
No longer shall the bodice, aptly laced,
From thy full bosom to thy slender waist 85
That air and harmony of shape express,
Fine by degrees and beautifully less:
Nor shall thy lower garment's artful pleat,
From thy fair side dependent to thy feet,
Arm their chaste beauties with a modest pride, 90
And double every charm they seek to hide.
The ambrosial plenty of thy shining hair,
Cropped off and lost, scarce lower than thy ear
Shall stand uncouth; a horseman's coat shall hide
Thy taper shape and comeliness of side; 95
The short trunk-hose shall show thy foot and knee
Licentious, and to common eyesight free;
And with a bolder stride and looser air,
Mingled with men, a man thou must appear . . .

ANON

'Robin Adair'

What's this dull town to me?
   Robin's not near.
What was't I wished to see,
   What wished to hear?
Where all the joy and mirth 5
Made this town heaven on earth?
Oh, they're all fled with thee,
   Robin Adair.

What made the assembly shine?
   Robin Adair. 10

What made the ball so fine?
   Robin was there.
What when the play was o'er,
What made my heart so sore?
Oh, it was parting with   15
   Robin Adair.

But now thou'rt cold to me,
   Robin Adair,
But now thou'rt cold to me,
   Robin Adair.   20
Yet he I loved so well
Still in my heart shall dwell;
Oh, I can ne'er forget
   Robin Adair.

SIR WALTER SCOTT

from The Lay of the Last Minstrel

CANTO II

1

If thou wouldst view fair Melrose aright,
Go visit it by the pale moonlight;
For the gay beams of lightsome day
Gild, but to flout, the ruins grey.
When the broken arches are black in night,   5
And each shafted oriel glimmers white;
When the cold light's uncertain shower
Streams on the ruined central tower;
When buttress and buttress, alternately,
Seem framed of ebon and ivory;   10
When silver edges the imagery,
And the scrolls that teach thee to live and die;

When distant Tweed is heard to rave,
And the owlet to hoot o'er the dead man's grave,
Then go – but go alone the while –   15
Then view St David's ruined pile
And, home returning, soothly swear
Was never scene so sad and fair!

                           2
Short halt did Deloraine make there;
Little recked he of the scene so fair;   20
With daggered hilt, on the wicket strong,
He struck full loud and struck full long.
The porter hurried to the gate –
'Who knocks so loud, and knocks so late?'
'From Branksome I,' the warrior cried;   25
And straight the wicket opened wide:
For Branksome's chiefs had in battle stood
        To fence the rights of fair Melrose,
And lands and livings many a rood
        Had gifted the shrine for their souls' repose.   30

                           3
Bold Deloraine his errand said;
The porter bent his humble head;
With torch in hand, and feet unshod,
And noiseless step, the path he trod,
The arched cloister far and wide   35
Rang to the warrior's clanking stride,
Till, stooping low his lofty crest,
He entered the cell of the ancient priest,
And lifted his barred aventayle,
To hail the Monk of St Mary's aisle.   40

                           4
'The Ladye of Branksome greets thee by me,
        Says, that the fated hour is come,
And that tonight I shall watch with thee,
        To win the treasure of the tomb.'
From sackcloth couch the monk arose,   45

With toil his stiffened limbs he reared;
A hundred years had flung their snows
On his thin locks and floating beard.

5

And strangely on the knight looked he,
    And his blue eyes gleamed wild and wide;   50
    'And darest thou, warrior, seek to see
    What heaven and hell alike would hide?
My breast in pelt of iron pent,
    With shirt of hair and scourge of thorn,
For threescore years, in penance spent,   55
    My knees these flinty stones have worn:
Yet all too little to atone
For knowing what should ne'er be known.
    Wouldst thou thy every future year
        In ceaseless prayer and penance drie,   60
    Yet wait thy latter end with fear –
        Then, daring warrior, follow me!'

6

'Penance, Father, will I none;
Prayer know I hardly one;
For mass or prayer I rarely tarry,   65
Save to patter an Ave Mary
When I ride on a Border foray.
Other prayer can I none;
So speed me my errand, and let me be gone.'

7

Again on the knight looked the churchman old,   70
    And again he sighed heavily;
For he had himself been a warrior bold,
    And fought in Spain and Italy.
And he thought on the days that were long since by,
When his limbs were strong and his courage was high;   75
Now, slow and faint, he led the way,
Where, cloistered round, the garden lay;

The pillared arches were over their head,
And beneath their feet were the bones of the dead.

8

Spreading herbs, and flowerets bright,   80
Glistened with the dew of night:
Nor herb nor floweret glistened there,
But was carved in the cloister arches as fair.
    The monk gazed long on the lovely moon,
        Then into the night he looked forth,   85
    And red and bright the streamers light
        Were dancing in the glowing north.
    So had he seen, in fair Castile,
        The youth in glittering squadrons start;
    Sudden the flying jennet wheel,   90
        And hurl the unexpected dart.
He knew, by the streamers that shot so bright
That spirits were riding the northern light.

9

By a steel-clenched postern door
    They entered now the chancel tall;   95
The darkened roof rose high aloof
    On pillars lofty, and light, and small:
The keystone that locked each ribbed aisle
    Was a fleur-de-lis or a quatrefoil.
The corbels were carved grotesque and grim,   100
And the pillars, with clustered shafts so trim,
With base and with capital flourished around,
Seemed bundles of lances which garlands had bound.

10

Full many a scutcheon and banner riven
Shook to the cold night wind of heaven   105
    Around the screenëd altar's pale;
And there the dying lamps did burn
Before thy low and lonely urn,
O gallant chief of Otterburn!
    And thine, dark knight of Liddesdale!   110
O fading honours of the dead!
O high ambition lowly laid!

11

The moon on the east oriel shone
Through slender shafts of shapely stone
    By foliaged tracery combined: 115
Thou wouldst have thought some fairy's hand
'Twixt poplars straight the osier wand,
    In many a freakish knot, had twined,
Then framed a spell when work was done,
And changed the willow wreaths to stone.   120
The silver light, so pale and faint,
Showed many a prophet and many a saint
    Whose image on the glass was dyed:
Full in the midst his cross of red
Triumphant Michael brandished,   125
    And trampled the apostate's pride.
The moonbeam kissed the holy pane,
And threw on the pavement a bloody stain.

12

They sat them down on a marble stone
    (A Scottish monarch slept below);   130
Thus spoke the monk in solemn tone:
    'I was not always a man of woe;
For paynim countries I have trod
And fought beneath the cross of God:
Now, strange to my eyes thine arms appear,   135
And their iron clang sounds strange to my ear.

13

'In these far climes it was my lot
To meet the wondrous Michael Scott,
    A wizard of such dreaded fame
That when, in Salamanca's cave,   140
Him listed his magic wand to wave,
    The bells would ring in Notre Dame!
Some of his skill he taught to me;
And, warrior, I could say to thee
The words that cleft Eildon hills in three,   145
    And bridled the Tweed with a curb of stone:

But to speak them were a deadly sin;
And for having but thought them my heart within
    A treble penance must be done.

14

'When Michael lay on his dying bed   150
His conscience was awakened:
He bethought him of his sinful deed,
And he gave me a sign to come with speed;
I was in Spain when the morning rose,
But I stood by his bed ere evening close.   155
The words may not again be said,
That he spoke to me, on his death-bed laid:
They would rend this abbey's massy nave,
And pile it in heaps above his grave.

15

'I swore to bury his mighty book   160
That never mortal mind might therein look;
And never to tell where it was hid,
Save at the chief of Branksome's need:
And, when that need was past and o'er,
Again the volume to restore.   165
I buried him on St Michael's night,
When the bell tolled one and the moon was bright,
And I dug his chamber among the dead,
When the floor of the chancel was stained red,
That his patron's cross might over him wave,   170
And scare the fiends from the wizard's grave.

16

'It was a night of woe and dread
When Michael in the tomb I laid!
Strange sounds along the chancel passed;
The banners waved without a blast' –   175
Still spoke the monk when the bell tolled one!
I tell you that a braver man
Than William of Deloraine, good at need,
Against a foe ne'er spurred a steed;

Yet somewhat was he chilled with dread,   180
And his hair did bristle upon his head.

17

'Lo, warrior, now the cross of red
Points to the grave of the mighty dead.
Within it burns a wondrous light
To chase the spirits that love the night: 185
That lamp shall burn unquenchably
Until the eternal doom shall be.'
Slow moved the monk to the broad flagstone
Which the bloody cross was traced upon:
He pointed to a secret nook;   190
An iron bar the warrior took;
And the monk made a sign with his withered hand
The grave's huge portal to expand.

18

With beating heart to the task he went;
His sinewy frame o'er the gravestone bent;   195
With bar of iron heaved amain
Till the toil-drops fell from his brows like rain:
It was by dint of passing strength
That he moved the massy stone at length.
I would you had been there to see   200
How the light broke forth so gloriously,
Streamed upward to the chancel roof,
And through the galleries far aloof!
No earthly flame blazed e'er so bright:
It shone like heaven's own blessed light   205
          And, issuing from the tomb,
Showed the monk's cowl and visage pale,
Danced on the dark-browed warrior's mail,
          And kissed his waving plume.

19

Before their eyes the wizard lay,   210
As if he had not been dead a day.
His hoary beard in silver rolled,

He seemed some seventy winters old;
 A palmer's amice wrapped him round,
 With a wrought Spanish baldric bound,   215
  Like a pilgrim from beyond the sea:
 His left hand held his book of might,
 A silver cross was in his right;
  The lamp was placed beside his knee.
High and majestic was his look,   220
At which the fellest fiends had shook,
And all unruffled was his face:
They trusted his soul had gotten grace.

20

Often had William of Deloraine
Rode through the battle's bloody plain,   225
And trampled down the warriors slain,
 And neither known remorse nor awe;
Yet now remorse and awe he owned.
His breath came thick, his head swam round,
 When this strange scene of death he saw;   230
Bewildered and unnerved he stood,
And the priest prayed fervently and loud:
With eyes averted prayed he;
He might not endure the sight to see
Of the man he loved so brotherly.   235

21

And when the priest his death-prayer had prayed
Thus unto Deloraine he said:
'Now speed thee what thou hast to do
Or, warrior, we may dearly rue;
For those thou mayest not look upon   240
Are gathering fast round the yawning stone!'
Then Deloraine in terror took
From the cold hand the mighty book,
With iron clasped, and with iron bound.
He thought, as he took it, the dead man frowned,   245
But the glare of the sepulchral light
Perchance had dazzled the warrior's sight.

22

When the huge stone sunk o'er the tomb
The night returned in double gloom;
For the moon had gone down, and the stars were few,   250
And, as the knight and priest withdrew
With wavering steps and dizzy brain,
They hardly might the postern gain.
'Tis said, as through the aisles they passed,
They heard strange noises on the blast;   255
And through the cloister galleries small
(Which at mid-height thread the chancel wall)
Loud sobs, and laughter louder, ran,
And voices unlike the voice of man,
As if the fiends kept holiday,   260
Because these spells were brought today.
I cannot tell how the truth may be;
I say the tale as 'twas said to me.

23

'Now hie thee hence,' the Father said,
'And when we are on death-bed laid,   265
Oh may Our Ladye, and sweet St John,
Forgive our souls for the deed we have done!'
    The monk returned him to his cell,
      And many a prayer and penance sped:
    When the convent met at the noontide bell   270
      The Monk of St Mary's aisle was dead!
Before the cross was the body laid,
With hands clasped fast as if still he prayed.

24

The knight breathed free in the morning wind,
And strove his hardihood to find: 275
He was glad when he passed the tombstones grey
Which girdle round the fair abbey,
For the mystic book, to his bosom pressed,
Felt like a load upon his breast,
And his joints, with nerves of iron twined,   280
Shook like the aspen leaves in wind.

Full fain was he when the dawn of day
Began to brighten the Cheviot grey;
He joyed to see the cheerful light,
And he said Ave Mary, as well he might.   285

25
The sun had brightened the Cheviot grey,
    The sun had brightened the Carter's side;
And soon beneath the rising day
    Smiled Branksome Towers and Teviot's tide.
The wild birds told their warbling tale,   290
    And wakened every flower that blows,
And peeped forth the violet pale,
    And spread her breast the mountain rose;
And lovelier than the rose so red,
    Yet paler than the violet pale,   295
She early left her sleepless bed,
    The fairest maid of Teviotdale.

26
Why does fair Margaret so early wake,
    And don her kirtle so hastily;
And the silken knots, which in hurry she would make,   300
    Why tremble her fingers to tie?
Why does she stop, and look often around,
    As she glides down the secret stair?
And why does she pat the shaggy bloodhound
    As he rises him up from his lair,   305
And, though she passes the postern alone,
Why is not the watchman's bugle blown?

27
The ladye steps in doubt and dread,
Lest her watchful mother hear her tread;
The ladye caresses the rough bloodhound   310
Lest his voice should waken the castle round;
The watchman's bugle is not blown
For he was her father's foster son;

And she glides through the greenwood at dawn of light
To meet Baron Henry, her own true knight.   315

28

The knight and ladye fair are met,
And under hawthorn's boughs are set:
A fairer pair were never seen
To meet beneath the hawthorn green.
He was stately, and young, and tall,   320
Dreaded in battle and loved in hall;
And she – when love, scarce-told, scarce hid,
Lent to her cheek a livelier red;
When the half sigh her swelling breast
Against the silken ribbon pressed;   325
When her blue eyes their secret told,
Though shaded by her locks of gold –
Where would you find the peerless fair
With Margaret of Branksome might compare?

29

And now, fair dames, methinks I see   330
You listen to my minstrelsy;
Your waving locks ye backward throw,
And sidelong bend your necks of snow.
Ye ween to hear a melting tale
Of two true lovers in a dale,   335
    And how the knight, with tender fire,
        To paint his tender passion strove;
    Swore he might at her feet expire,
        But never, never, cease to love;
And how she blushed, and how she sighed,   340
And, half consenting, half denied,
And said that she would die a maid –
Yet, might the bloody feud be stayed,
Henry of Cranstoun, and only he,
Margaret of Branksome's choice should be.   345

30

Alas, fair dames, your hopes are vain!
My harp has lost the enchanting strain:
    Its lightness would my age reprove.

My hairs are grey, my limbs are old,
My heart is dead, my veins are cold: 350
    I may not, must not, sing of love.

31

Beneath an oak, mossed o'er by eld,
The baron's dwarf his courser held,
    And led his crested helm and spear:
That dwarf was scarce an earthly man,   355
If the tales were true that of him ran
    Through all the Border far and near.
'Twas said, when the baron a-hunting rode
Through Reedsdale's glens, but rarely trod,
He heard a voice cry, 'Lost! lost! lost!'   360
And, like a tennis ball by racquet tossed,
    A leap of thirty feet and three
Made from the gorse this elfin shape,
Distorted like some dwarfish ape,
    And lighted at Lord Cranstoun's knee.   365
Lord Cranstoun was some whit dismayed:
'Tis said that five good mile he rade
    To rid him of his company;
But, where he rode one mile, the dwarf ran four,
And the dwarf was first at the castle door.   370

32

Use lessens marvels, it is said.
This elvish dwarf with the baron stayed:
Little he ate, and less he spoke,
Nor mingled with the menial flock,
And oft apart his arms he tossed,   375
And often muttered 'Lost! lost! lost!'
    He was waspish, arch, and litherly,
    But well Lord Cranstoun served he,
And he of his service was full fain;
For once he had been ta'en or slain   380
    An it had not been for his ministry.
All between Home and Hermitage
Talked of Lord Cranstoun's goblin page.

33

For the baron went on pilgrimage,
And took with him this elvish page   385
    To Mary's chapel of the Lowes;
For there, beside Our Ladye's lake,
An offering he had sworn to make,
    And he would pay his vows.
But the Ladye of Branksome gathered a band   390
Of the best that would ride at her command:
    The trysting place was Newark Lee.
Wat of Harden came thither amain,
And thither came John of Thirlestane,
And thither came William of Deloraine;   395
    They were three hundred spears and three.
Through Douglas burn, up Yarrow stream,
Their horses prance, their lances gleam.
They came to St Mary's lake ere day,
But the chapel was void, and the baron away.   400
They burned the chapel for very rage,
And cursed Lord Cranstoun's goblin page.

34

And now, in Branksome's good green wood,
As under an aged oak he stood,
The baron's courser pricks his ears,   405
As if a distant voice he hears.
The dwarf waves his long, lean arm on high,
And signs to the lovers to part and fly;
No time was then to vow or sigh.
Fair Margaret through the hazel grove   410
Flew like the startled cushat-dove:
The dwarf the stirrup held and rein;
Vaulted the knight on his steed amain
And, pondering deep that morning's scene,
Rode eastward through the hawthorns green.   415

While thus he poured the lengthened tale
The minstrel's voice began to fail;

Full slily smiled the observant page,
And gave the withered hand of age
A goblet crowned with mighty wine,   420
The blood of Velez' scorched vine.
He raised the silver cup on high
And, while the big drop filled his eye,
Prayed God to bless the duchess long
And all who cheered a son of song.   425
The attending maidens smiled to see
How long, how deep, how zealously,
The precious juice the minstrel quaffed;
And he, emboldened by the draught,
Looked gaily back to them and laughed.   430
The cordial nectar of the bowl
Swelled his old veins, and cheered his soul:
A lighter, livelier prelude ran
Ere thus his tale again began . . .

from Marmion

CANTO VI

30

O Woman! in our hours of ease,
Uncertain, coy, and hard to please,
And variable as the shade
By the light quivering aspen made;
When pain and anguish wring the brow,   5
 A ministering angel, thou! –
Scarce were the piteous accents said,
When, with the baron's casque, the maid
    To the nigh streamlet ran:
Forgot were hatred, wrongs and fears –   10
The plaintive voice alone she hears,
    Sees but the dying man.
She stooped her by the runnel's side,

But in abhorrence backward drew;
For, oozing from the mountain's side   15
Where raged the war, a dark-red tide
 Was curdling in the streamlet blue.
Where shall she turn? – behold her mark
 A little fountain cell,
Where water, clear as diamond spark,   20
 In a stone basin fell.
Above, some half-worn letters say,
𝔇𝔯𝔦𝔫𝔨. 𝔴𝔢𝔞𝔯𝔶. 𝔭𝔦𝔩𝔤𝔯𝔦𝔪. 𝔡𝔯𝔦𝔫𝔨 𝔞𝔫𝔡. 𝔭𝔯𝔞𝔶.
𝔉𝔬𝔯. 𝔱𝔥𝔢. 𝔨𝔦𝔫𝔡. 𝔰𝔬𝔲𝔩. 𝔬𝔣. 𝔖𝔶𝔟𝔦𝔩. 𝔊𝔯𝔢𝔶.
 𝔚𝔥𝔬 𝔟𝔲𝔦𝔩𝔱. 𝔱𝔥𝔦𝔰. 𝔠𝔯𝔬𝔰𝔰. 𝔞𝔫𝔡. 𝔴𝔢𝔩𝔩.   25
She filled the helm, and back she hied,
And with surprise and joy espied
 A monk supporting Marmion's head:
A pious man, whom duty brought
To dubious verge of battle fought   30
 To shrive the dying, bless the dead...

38

I do not rhyme to that dull elf
Who cannot image to himself
That all through Flodden's dismal night
Wilton was foremost in the fight;   35
That, when brave Surrey's steed was slain
'Twas Wilton mounted him again;
'Twas Wilton's brand that deepest hewed
Amid the spearmen's stubborn wood.
Unnamed by Holinshed or Hall,   40
He was the living soul of all,
That, after fight, his faith made plain,
He won his rank and lands again,
And charged the old paternal shield
With bearings won on Flodden field.   45
Nor sing I to that simple maid
To whom it must in terms be said,
That king and kinsmen did agree
To bless fair Clara's constancy;
Who cannot, unless I relate,   50
Paint to her mind the bridal's state;
That Wolsey's voice the blessing spoke,

More, Sands, and Denny passed the joke;
That bluff King Hal the curtain drew,
And Catherine's hand the stocking threw;   55
And afterwards, for many a day,
That it was held enough to say
In blessing to the wedded pair:
'Love they like Wilton and his Clare!'

from The Lady of the Lake

CANTO II

17

Ever, as on they bore, more loud
And louder rung the pibroch proud.
At first the sound, by distance tame,
Mellowed along the waters came
And, lingering long by cape and bay,   5
Wailed every harsher note away;
Then, bursting bolder on the ear,
The clan's shrill Gathering they could hear:
Those thrilling sounds that call the might
Of old Clan Alpine to the fight.   10
Thick beat the rapid notes, as when
The mustering hundreds shake the glen
And, hurrying at the signal dread,
The battered earth returns their tread.
Then prelude light, of livelier tone,   15
Expressed their merry marching on
Ere peal of closing battle rose,
With mingled outcry, shrieks and blows,
And mimic din of stroke and ward,
As broad sword upon target jarred;   20
And groaning pause, ere yet again,
Condensed, the battle yelled amain;
The rapid charge, the rallying shout,

Retreat borne headlong into rout,
And bursts of triumph, to declare   25
Clan Alpine's conquest – all were there.
Nor ended thus the strain; but slow,
Sunk in a moan prolonged and low,
And changed the conquering clarion swell,
For wild lament o'er those that fell.   30

18

The war-pipes ceased; but lake and hill
Were busy with their echoes still;
And, when they slept, a vocal strain
Bade their hoarse chorus wake again,
While loud a hundred clansmen raise   35
Their voices in their chieftain's praise.
Each boatman, bending to his oar,
With measured sweep the burden bore
In such wild cadence as the breeze
Makes through December's leafless trees.   40
The chorus first could Allan know,
'Roderick Vich Alpine, ho! iro!'
And near, and nearer, as they rowed,
Distinct the martial ditty flowed...

21

With all her joyful female band   45
Had Lady Margaret sought the strand:
Loose on the breeze their tresses flew,
And high their snowy arms they threw
As echoing back with shrill acclaim,
And chorus wild, the chieftain's name;   50
While, prompt to please, with mother's art,
The darling passion of his heart,
The dame called Ellen to the strand,
To greet her kinsman ere he land:
'Come, loiterer, come! A Douglas thou,   55
And shun to wreathe a victor's brow?'
Reluctantly and slow, the maid
The unwelcome summoning obeyed
And, when a distant bugle rung,

In the mid-path aside she sprung: 60
'List, Allan Bane! From mainland cast
I hear my father's signal blast.
Be ours,' she said, 'the skiff to guide,
And waft him from the mountain side.'
Then, like a sunbeam, swift and bright,   65
She darted from her shallop light
And, eagerly while Roderick scanned,
For her dear form, his mother's band,
The islet far behind her lay,
And she had landed in the bay.   70

22

Some feelings are to mortals given,
With less of earth in them than heaven:
And if there be a human tear
From passion's dross refined and clear,
A tear so limpid and so meek,   75
It would not stain an angel's cheek,
'Tis that which pious fathers shed
Upon a duteous daughter's head!
And as the Douglas to his breast
His darling Ellen closely pressed,   80
Such holy drops her tresses steeped,
Though 'twas a hero's eye that weeped,
Nor while on Ellen's faltering tongue
Her filial welcomes crowded hung,
Marked she, that fear (affection's proof)   85
Still held a graceful youth aloof;
No! not till Douglas named his name,
Although the youth was Malcolm Graeme . . .

ROBERT SOUTHEY

from The Poet's Pilgrimage to Waterloo

PROEM

Once more I see thee, Skiddaw! once again
 Behold thee in thy majesty serene,
Where like the bulwark of this favoured plain,
 Alone thou standest, monarch of the scene . . .
Thou glorious mountain, on whose ample breast   5
The sunbeams love to play, the vapours love to rest!

Once more, O Derwent, to thy aweful shores
 I come, insatiate of the accustomed sight;
And listening as the eternal torrent roars,
 Drink in with eye and ear a fresh delight: 10
For I have wandered far by land and sea,
In all my wanderings still remembering thee.

Twelve years (how large a part of man's brief day)
 Nor idly, nor ingloriously spent,
Of evil and of good have held their way,   15
 Since first upon thy banks I pitched my tent.
Hither I came in manhood's active prime,
And here my head hath felt the touch of time.

Heaven hath with goodly increase blest me here,
 Where childless and oppressed with grief I came; 20
With voice of fervent thankfulness sincere
 Let me the blessings which are mine proclaim:
Here I possess, . . . what more should I require?
Books, children, leisure, . . . all my heart's desire.

O joyful hour, when to our longing home   25
 The long-expected wheels at length drew nigh!
When first the sound went forth, 'They come, they come!'
 And hope's impatience quickened every eye!
'Never had man whom heaven would heap with bliss
More glad return, more happy hour than this.'   30

Aloft on yonder bench, with arms dispread,
    My boy stood, shouting there his father's name,
Waving his hat around his happy head;
    And there, a younger group, his sisters came:
Smiling they stood with looks of pleased surprise,   35
While tears of joy were seen in elder eyes.

Soon each and all came crowding round to share
    The cordial greeting, the beloved sight;
What welcomings of hand and lip were there!
    And when those overflowings of delight   40
Subsided to a sense of quiet bliss,
Life hath no purer, deeper happiness...

JAMES THOMSON

The Seasons

from Spring

    But happy they – the happiest of their kind –
Whom gentler stars unite and, in one fate,
Their hearts, their fortunes, and their beings blend.
'Tis not the coarser tie of human laws,
Unnatural oft, and foreign to the mind,   5
That binds their peace, but harmony itself,
Attuning all their passions unto love,
Where friendship full-exerts her softest power,
Perfect esteem enlivened by desire
Ineffable and sympathy of soul,   10
Thought meeting thought, and will preventing will,
With boundless confidence: for naught but love
Can answer love, and render bliss secure.
Let him, ungenerous, who, alone intent
To bless himself, from sordid parents buys   15
The loathing virgin, in eternal care

Well-merited consume his nights and days;
Let barbarous nations, whose inhuman love
Is wild, desire fierce as the suns they feel;
Let eastern tyrants from the light of heaven   20
Seclude their bosom slaves, meanly possessed
Of a mere lifeless, violated form;
While those whom love cements in holy faith
And equal transport free as nature live,
Disdaining fear. What is the world to them,   25
Its pomp, its pleasure, and its nonsense all,
Who in each other clasp whatever fair
High fancy forms, and lavish hearts can wish?
Something than beauty dearer, should they look
Or on the mind or mind-illumined face: 30
Truth, goodness, honour, harmony and love –
The richest bounty of indulgent heaven!
Meantime a smiling offspring rises round,
And mingles both their graces. By degrees
The human blossom blows; and every day,   35
Soft as it rolls along, shows some new charm –
The father's lustre and the mother's bloom.
Then infant reason grows apace, and calls
For the kind hand of an assiduous care:
Delightful task! to rear the tender thought,   40
To teach the young idea how to shoot,
To pour the fresh instruction o'er the mind,
To breathe the enlivening spirit, and to fix
The generous purpose in the glowing breast.
Oh, speak the joy, ye whom the sudden tear   45
Surprises often while you look around,
And nothing strikes your eye but sights of bliss,
All various Nature pressing on the heart –
An elegant sufficiency, content,
Retirement, rural quiet, friendship, books,   50
Ease and alternate labour, useful life,
Progressive virtue, and approving heaven!
These are the matchless joys of virtuous love,
And thus their moments fly. The seasons thus,
As ceaseless round a jarring world they roll,   55
Still find them happy. And consenting Spring

Sheds her own rosy garland on their heads,
Till evening comes at last, serene and mild;
When, after the long vernal day of life,
Enamoured more, as more remembrance swells 60
With many a proof of recollected love,
Together down they sink in social sleep;
Together freed, their gentle spirits fly
To scenes where love and bliss immortal reign.

WILLIAM WHITEHEAD

The *Je ne scai quoi*

Yes, I'm in love, I feel it now,
    And Celia has undone me!
And yet I'll swear I can't tell how
    The pleasing plague stole on me.

'Tis not her face which love creates, 5
    For there no graces revel;
'Tis not her shape, for there the Fates
    Have rather been uncivil.

'Tis not her air for, sure, in that
    There's nothing more than common; 10
And all her sense is only chat,
    Like any other woman.

Her voice, her touch, might give the alarm –
    'Twas both, perhaps, or neither;
In short, 'twas that provoking charm 15
    Of Celia altogether.

Notes

References to JA's letters are to *Jane Austen's Letters*, ed. Deirdre Le Faye, 3rd edn (Oxford, New York: Oxford University Press, 1995).

Jane Austen

From the *Juvenilia* (1787–93)
Song (1); Epitaph; Song (2) From *Frederic and Elfrida, A Novel* (in *Volume the First*). *Song (2)* 4 **fess**: elated.

Song From *Henry and Eliza, A Novel* (in *Volume the First*).

Ode to Pity Concludes *Volume the First*. 5 **Philomel**: nightingale. 8 **brawling**: flowing noisily. 13 **cot**: small cottage; **grot**: grotto.

Song (1); Song (2) From *The First Act of a Comedy* (in *Volume the Second*).

'This Little Bag' (1792) Written to accompany a gift of a needlework bag to Mary Lloyd (who married James Austen in 1797).

Lines ... niece ... (1806) Sent to JA's niece Fanny Austen on the marriage of Francis Austen to Mary Gibson, daughter of Mr and Mrs John Gibson of the High Street, Ramsgate. The marriage took place at Ramsgate.

'Oh! Mr Best ...' (1806) 1 **Mr Best**: unidentified. 10 **posting**: i.e., distance. 11 **stouter**: healthier; stronger. 19 **Richard's pills**: a joke at the expense of a name JA disliked, not a genuine brand. 24 **Martha Lloyd**: (1765–1843), elder sister of Mary (*'This Little Bag'* note), who lived with the Austens and became Francis Austen's second wife in 1828, some years after the death of Mary. An aunt on her mother's side lived at **Speen (36)**. 37 **Morton's wife**: friend of Martha Lloyd.

On Sir Home Popham's sentence (1807) Sir Home Riggs Popham was tried at Portsmouth in March 1807 charged with having, without orders, withdrawn his squadron from the Cape of Good Hope. He was reprimanded but subsequently had a good naval career. There was a small family connection through Francis Austen.

To Miss Bigg ... (1808) **Title:** Catherine Bigg, a childhood friend of JA, of Manydown Park, Hampshire. Her young brother, Harris Bigg-Wither, had proposed to JA in December 1802 and been refused **1 Cambric:** fine white linen.

To the Memory of Mrs Lefroy ... (1808) **Title:** Anne Brydges (1749–1804) married the Rev. I. P. G. Lefroy in 1778; she died in a riding accident. One of her sons, Benjamin, married Anna Austen (daughter of James) in 1814. **13 Johnson ... Hamilton:** Boswell, *Life of Johnson*, 20 December 1784 quoting W. G. Hamilton. **22 to thee:** compared to thee. **36 but:** only.

'Alas, poor Brag!' ... (1809) In a letter to Cassandra of 17 January 1809. The letter to her of 10 January 1809 comments on the preference of speculation over brag at Godmersham, one of Edward Austen's houses. **1 brag:** card game like poker; the brag is the challenge to opponents to produce cards of the same value as the challenger's. **5 speculation:** card game: see *Mansfield Park*, II.7.

'My dearest Frank' (1809) Verse-letter sent to Francis Austen dated 26 July 1809 (see notes to *Lines ... niece* ... and *'Oh! Mr Best ...'* above). **2 a boy:** Francis junior was born on 12 July 1809. **4 Mary Jane:** born on 27 April 1807. **18 Bet:** the nurserymaid; **bide:** stay long. **43 Chawton:** Mrs Austen and daughters had moved to Chawton Cottage on 7 July, on Edward Austen's estate. **50 Charles and Fanny:** Charles Austen had married Frances Palmer in 1807.

'In Measured Verse ...' (?1810) **2 Anna:** Edward's impulsive daughter, who had been sent by her parents – annoyed at her having broken her engagement to the Rev. Michael Terry – to stay at Chawton Cottage in the summer of 1810.

'I've a Pain in my Head' (1811) **2 Beckford:** Maria Beckford, unmarried daughter of Francis Beckford of Basing Park, Hampshire. **12 calomel:** a powder of mercurous chloride – used as a purgative!

On ... the Marriage of 'Mr Gell ... to Miss Gill' (1811) An announcement in the *Hampshire Telegraph and Sussex Chronicle*, 25 February 1811, stated: 'On Saturday was married, Mr Gell, of Eastbourne, to Miss Gill, of Well Street, Hackney.' **6, 8 eyes, ease:** punning (as MS variants make clear) on 'i's and 'e's (Gill becomes Gell).

'I am in a Dilemma'; 'Between Session and Session' (1811) Both in a letter to Cassandra of 30 April 1811, the first preceded by 'Oh! yes, I remember Miss Emma Plumbtree's *local* consequence perfectly'; the second after: 'I congratulate Edward on the Weald of Kent Canal Bill being put off till another session . . . There is always something to be hoped from Delay.' **Between Session and Session 2 prepossession:** the speculative buying of land in expectation of the passing of the Bill, which would arouse local opposition.

'When Stretched on One's Bed' (1811) **17 stews:** the still-fashionable ragout. **23 corse:** corpse.

On the Marriage of Miss Camilla Wallop ... (1812) The letter to Martha Lloyd of 29 November 1812 mentions 'the 4 lines on Miss Wallop which I sent you were all my own,' adding: 'James afterwards suggested what I thought a great improvement.' Camilla Wallop married the Rev. Henry Wake. **4 Wake:** night-time vigil before a festival.

Riddles Undated; first published 1895. Solutions: hemlock; agent; banknote.

To Miss—. Charade (?1814) In *Emma* (1816), I.9. Solution: courtship.

Written at Winchester ... (1817) JA spent her last few months being looked after at Winchester. She composed these verses three days before her death on 18 July 1817. **1 Winchester races:** on Worthy Down, the course was a particular favourite of Charles II. **3 St Swithin:** Bishop of Winchester (d. 862); the removal of his remains from his grave outside the Old Minster to a shrine inside on 15 July 971 was, it was said, accompanied by a storm, thus giving rise to the legend that if it rains on St Swithin's day it will rain for forty days. **4 William of Wykeham:** Bishop of Winchester and chancellor of England, 1367–1404; major contributor to the cathedral; founder of Winchester College and New College, Oxford. **11 the**

palace: Wolvesey Castle; it was destroyed in the Civil War. **13 Venta:** the Roman name for the city was Venta Belgarum.

James Beattie (1735–1803)

The Hermit (complete) JA quotes l.25 to announce the arrival of evening in a letter to Cassandra of 23–4 September 1813. **10 Philomela:** raped by her brother-in-law, Tereus, who also ripped out her tongue, she fled from him and escaped by being turned into a nightingale; she became an emblem of the poet. **13 lay:** song. **45 Truth . . . Mercy:** Psalm 85:10.

Isaac Hawkins Browne (1705–60)

A Pipe of Tobacco; Imitation 5
(complete); from Dodsley's *Collection of Poems in Six Volumes* (London, 1775), II.285 In *Mansfield Park*, I.17, Mary Crawford quotes, then parodies, the opening lines of this imitation of Alexander Pope when talking ironically of the 'mighty things' expected of Sir Thomas Bertram's return from the West Indies: 'Blest knight! whose dictatorial looks dispense/To children affluence, to Rushworth sense'. **2 templars:** barristers. **3 Dodona:** site of an oracle of Zeus, where prophecies were made from oak trees and wild doves. **9 cits:** contemptuous for citizen, meaning tradesman not gentleman. **11 beer:** joking alternative for inspirational wine: see Pope, *Epistle to Dr Arbuthnot*, l.15. **14 piddling:** trifling. **16 beau:** dandy. **20 unexcised:** increase in tobacco duty was a controversial issue at the time.

Robert Burns (1759–96)

He is mentioned in *Sanditon*, ch. 7, where Sir Edward, in a bravura display of acquaintance with modern poets, mentions the 'pathos to madden one' in 'Burns' lines to his Mary'; and Charlotte replies that she has read some Burns but finds that the 'irregularities' of his life affect her belief in his sincerity: 'He felt, and he wrote, and he forgot.' I have printed the Mary poems Sir Edward might have had in mind.

Mary Morison **5 stour:** storm; adversity. **10 gaed:** proceeded. **13 braw:** splendid.

Highland Mary **1 braes:** hills. **4 drumlie:** muddy. **9 birk:** birch tree. **13 Hours:** companions of Venus, goddess of love, they represented the seasons. **21 fell:** cruel.

George Gordon, Lord Byron (1788–1824)

The favourite (along with Scott) of the sentimental (i.e., emotional, 'feeling') and enthusiastic Captain Benwick in *Persuasion*. In I.11 he tries to ascertain whether Scott's *Marmion* or *Lady of the Lake* are preferable to Byron's *Giaour* and *Bride of Abydos* and is reported as quoting Byron's 'impassioned descriptions of hopeless agony; he repeated, with such tremulous feeling, the various lines which imaged a broken heart, or a mind destroyed by wretchedness, that [Anne] ventured to hope he did not read only poetry.' I have selected passages which JA may have had in mind. (In I.12 Benwick again talks of Scott and Byron; and in II.6 Anne supposes that, on their marriage, Benwick will learn cheerfulness from Louisa, and she enthusiasm for Scott and Byron from him.) [B] = Byron's own note.

The Giaour (1813), ll. 1130 to end with some omissions (marked ...; spaced dots are as original and indicated its fragmentary nature). **Title: The Giaour:** Turkish word for Christian. (The tale concerns Leila, a female slave, who was drowned in the sea for infidelity and avenged by her Venetian lover, who now confesses. It embodies the mixture of oriental and 'gothic' taste popular at the time.) **16 Looks ... relief:** the monk's sermon is omitted . . . [B]. **43 symar:** a shroud [B].

The Bride of Abydos (1813) The extract sufficiently conveys the story of hopeless and forbidden love. **6 Niobé:** her grief turned her to stone when her children were killed on the orders of Latona for having boasted that they were more beautiful than Latona's. **55 wul-wulleh:** the death-song of the Turkish women. The 'silent slaves' are the men . . . [B].

The Corsair (1814) As they proceed to the Cobb at Lyme, 'Anne found Captain Benwick again drawing near her. Lord Byron's "dark blue seas" [*Corsair*, l.1] could not fail of being brought forward by their present view . . .' (in *Letters*, 5 March 1814, JA tells Cassandra 'I have read the Corsair, mended my petticoat . . .'). **26 recks:** matters.

Thomas Campbell (1777–1844)

The Pleasures of Hope (1799), II, ll.375–406 Another of Sir Edward's poets in *Sanditon*, ch. 7 (see **Burns** note above): as he bombards Charlotte with quotations and opinions on poets, he enthuses that 'Campbell in his *Pleasures of Hope* has touched the extreme of our sensations – "Like Angel's visits, few and far between" ' (quoting l.378; l.4 of the present text). The lines come from near the end of the poem, where Hope is argued to offer us promise of an after-life. **30 mould:** earth, dust.

William Cowper (1731–1800)

One of JA's real favourites, the proposed purchase of his works is mentioned in a letter to Cassandra, 25 November 1798, and in a letter to her dated 18 December 1798 she notes that 'my Father reads Cowper to us in the evening, to which I listen when I can.' In *Sense and Sensibility*, Edward is culpable for reading Cowper 'with such impenetrable calmness, such dreadful indifference' (I.3); in I.10 Willoughby admires Cowper (along with Scott) 'as he ought'; and in I.17 Edward refers to Marianne's passion for 'Thomson, Cowper, Scott'.

Truth (1782) 'Mr Parker of Sanditon' applies l.334 (l.34 of this text) to Brinshore when Mr Heywood confesses to never having heard of the place (*Sanditon*, end of ch. 1) **4 Voltaire:** pseudonym of the French sceptical philosopher and satirist François Marie Arouet (1694–1778).

Verses . . . by Alexander Selkirk . . . (1782) Towards the end of her letter to Cassandra dated 23 September 1813, JA remarks that she is alone in the library, 'mistress of all I survey', and could go on to repeat the whole poem without offending anyone. **Title:** Selkirk (1676–1721) was left on the desert island of Juan Fernandez from 1704 to 1709 at his own request. He was the inspiration for Defoe's Robinson Crusoe. **4 I am lord . . . brute:** ironic reminder of Adam in Eden (Genesis 1:28). **19 Oh . . . dove:** Psalm 55:6 **31 knell:** bell tolled to mark a death or funeral.

Epitaph on a Hare (1784) The letter to Cassandra, 3 November 1813, refers to Cowper and tame hares in connection with fondness for the country (in contrast to Dr Johnson's love of London). Cowper had published an essay on his three pet hares in the *Gentleman's Magazine*, June 1784; this *Epitaph* was first published in the December issue.

The Task (1785)
Book I, The Sofa, ll.307–54 Fanny quotes II.338–9 (ll.32–3 of this text) to Edmund when she hears of Rushworth's plans to 'improve' Sotherton by cutting down its avenue of trees (*Mansfield Park*, I.6). **2 peculiar:** particular. **36 awful:** awe-inspiring.

Book IV, The Winter Evening, ll.267–97 In *Emma*, III.5, Mr Knightley suspects Frank Churchill of having a secret understanding with Jane Fairfax, 'unless it were like Cowper and his fire at twilight, "Myself creating what I saw" ' (l.290; 1.24 of the present text). **3–4 he ... Goliath:** 1 Samuel 17: 4–5. **20 ludicrous:** frivolous. **26–9 The sooty ... approach:** compare Coleridge, 'Frost at Midnight', ll.15–43; Coleridge's note to l.15 reads: 'In all parts of the kingdom these films are called *strangers* and supposed to portend the arrival of some absent friend.'

Book VI, The Winter Walk at Noon, ll.140–56 In the letter to Cassandra of 8 February 1807 JA writes of the shrubs they must get for the new garden: 'I could not do without a Syringa, for the sake of Cowper's line. – We talk also of a Laburnam' (see ll.10–11 of the present text). **11 syringa:** originally the mock-orange, but since Linnaeus' classification (1735), the lilac.

Tirocinium (1785), ll.537–76 In *Mansfield Park*, III.14, Fanny, staying with her parents in Portsmouth, adapts *Tirocinium*, l.562 (l.26 of my extract) as she realises how much she wants to be back home at Mansfield: ' "With what intense desire she wants her home," was continually on her tongue, as the truest description of a yearning which she could not suppose any schoolboy's bosom to feel more keenly'. **Title:** Latin for raw youth or early beginnings. **6 Vestris:** the French male dancer Auguste Vestris (1760–1842), a favourite of Marie Antoinette. Cowper mentions him in the essay on his pet hares (*Epitaph on a Hare* note above). **7 ingenuous:** honourable; of a noble disposition. **10 Aesop and Phaedrus:** Aesop, the sixth-century BC writer of fables; Phaedrus, of whom nothing is known, wrote Latin fables. Other fabulists to whom children were introduced included Anianus and Barlandus.

George Crabbe (1754–1832)

Tales, (1812)
Tale 3, The Gentleman Farmer In a letter to Cassandra of 15–16 September 1813, JA writes of a theatre visit: 'I was particularly disappointed at seeing nothing of Mr Crabbe. I felt sure of him when I saw that the

boxes were fitted up with Crimson velvet.' Her allusion is to l.59 of *Tale 3* (l.41 of my extract); I quote ll.19–60. (In other letters – of 21 October and 6 November 1813 – she seems to allude to the preface to Crabbe's *The Borough*; and records how a Miss Lee 'admires Crabbe as she ought'.)
Tale 11, Edward Shore In *Mansfield Park*. I.16, Edmund notices that Fanny has 'Crabbe's *Tales* and the *Idler*, at hand, to relieve [her]' if she tires of reading Lord Macartney's *Journal of the Embassy to China* (1807). Her upset at having just learned from him of his intention to act in the play *Lovers' Vows* – 'was he not deceiving himself? Was he not wrong? Alas! it was all Miss Crawford's doing' – suggests that JA might, with gentle irony, have had Crabbe's *Tale 11* in mind: it certainly reflects in alarmist form the fears Fanny seems to be entertaining about the apparently moral Edmund. (The Edward of the *Tale* ends up seducing his best friend's wife, then descending through dissipation into lunacy!) I quote ll.1–70. **1 Genius:** natural inclination, especially (though not necessarily) of an exalted type. **15 Samson:** Judges 13–16 (another victim of a woman).

David Garrick (1717–79)

A Riddle Mr Woodhouse quotes the first stanza of this riddle in *Emma*, I.9, and Emma tells him that she has already 'copied it from the *Elegant Extracts*', and identifies it as Garrick's. The official answer is the chimney sweeper; though the *double entendre* on Fanny (= vagina), together with other innuendoes, suggests the alternative answer, penis (and hence an insight into Mr Woodhouse's youthful self).

John Gay (1685–1732)

Fables (1727), **Fable 50, *The Hare and Many Friends*** JA mentions this fable twice: in *Northanger Abbey*, I.1, where the young Catherine learns it 'as quickly as any girl in England'; and in *Emma*, III.16, when Mrs Elton quotes ll.41–2 without, however, being able to recall the source of the quotation. Based on the proverb, 'have but few friends though much acquaintance.' **29 puss:** common name for a hare. **40 barley mow:** stack of barley.

Oliver Goldsmith (1730–74)

'When Lovely Woman . . .' From *The Vicar of Wakefield* (1766), ch. 24: Olivia sings it to her family while sitting on the bank where she first met her seducer. In *Emma*, III.9, the author remarks, on the death of Mrs Churchill: 'Goldsmith tells us, that when lovely woman stoops to folly, she has nothing to do but to die; and when she stoops to be disagreeable, it is equally to be recommended as a clearer of ill-fame.' (Earlier, at *Emma*, I.4, Harriet, attempting to recommend the farmer, Robert Martin, 'knows he has read the *Vicar of Wakefield*'.)

Thomas Gray (1716–71)

Elegy . . . (1751) From this poem Catherine Morland, as part of her training for being a heroine, learns 'Many a flower is born to blush unseen,/ And waste its fragrance on the desert air' (misquoting ll. 55–6): *Northanger Abbey*, I.1. In *Emma*, II.15, Mrs Elton misquotes the same lines as she affirms that Jane Fairfax must be 'brought forward'. **1 curfew:** evening bell, often rung at eight or nine p.m. **22 ply:** apply herself busily to. **26 glebe:** earth; field. **41 storied:** inscribed with memorial records. **48 Or . . . lyre:** a potential poet. **52 genial:** creative; warm. **57 Hampden:** John Hampden, one of the five members of the House of Commons, the attempted arrest of whom by Charles I in January 1642 led to the Civil War.

James Merrick (1720–69)

The Chameleon In Dodsley (see **Browne** above), V. 223–5. In *Volume the First*, 'Jack and Alice', ch. 3: 'The dispute at length grew so hot on the part of Alice, that "From words she almost came to blows" ' with Lady Williams (quoting l.46 of the poem). **2 spark:** fop.

John Milton (1608–74)

L'Allegro (1645), ll.115 to the end. The pretentious Mrs Elton quotes *L'Allegro*, ll.125–6 (11–12 in present text) in *Emma*, II.18 ('because things . . . did not proceed with all the rapidity which suited his feelings, he was apt

... to exclaim that he was sure at this rate it would be *May* before Hymen's saffron robe would be put on for us!'). **Title:** the happy man (companion poem to *Il Penseroso*, the thoughtful melancholic). **6 weeds:** clothes; **triumphs:** pageants. **7 store:** abundance. **11 Hymen:** god of marriage. **18 Jonson:** Ben (1572–1637), dramatist and poet; **sock:** slipper, emblem of comedy. **22 Lydian:** the relaxing musical mode. **31 Orpheus:** mythical poet, whose wife died and went to Pluto's infernal kingdom.

Paradise Lost (1667) in *Mansfield Park*, I.4, Henry, after Mary has accused him to Mrs Grant of being a flirt, says, 'Nobody can think more highly of the matrimonial state than myself. I consider the blessing of a wife as most justly described in those discreet lines of the poet, "Heaven's *last* best gift" ' (*Paradise Lost*, V.19). **2 orient:** eastern; bright. **16 Flora:** goddess of flowers. **40 night-warbling bird:** nightingale.

Thomas Moss

The Beggar's Petition or *The Poor Man's Prayer* (1766)
Catherine, as a young girl, 'was often inattentive, and occasionally stupid. Her mother was three months in teaching her to repeat the "Beggar's Petition" ' (*Northanger Abbey*, I.1). **5 Chatham:** William Pitt, Earl of Chatham (1708–78).

Alexander Pope (1688–1744)

An Essay on Criticism (1711), l.215 (l.1 of my extract) is quoted by Mr Elliot in *Persuasion*, II.4 ('a little learning is by no means a dangerous thing in good company'). **2 Pierian spring:** fountain of the Muses.

Elegy (1717) *Northanger Abbey*, I.1, quotes l.57 among the things learned from poetry suitable for a heroine ('she learned to censure those who "bear about the mockery of woe" '). **8 Roman's part:** suicide. **9 reversion:** inheritance. **41 Furies:** goddesses of vengeance. **52 decent:** comely. **59 Loves:** Cupids. **66 blow:** bloom.

An Essay on Man (1733–4), I.294 (l.36 of my extract) is parodied in *Letters*, 26 October 1813 (' "What ever is, is best." There has been one infallible Pope in the world'). I quote ll.259–94. **20 seraph ... burns:** traditionally, with the love of God.

Matthew Prior (1664–1721)

Henry and Emma (1708) In *Persuasion*, I.12, Anne 'endeavoured to be composed, and to be just. Without emulating the feelings of an Emma towards her Henry, she would have attended on Louisa with a zeal above the common claims of regard, for [Captin Wentworth's] sake . . .'. I quote ll. 344–442 to exemplify what JA had in mind. **1 Thalestris:** queen of the Amazons. **4 Bonduca:** Boadicea. **17 lawn:** fine linen.

'Robin Adair' Jane Fairfax plays the air on her new pianoforte in *Emma*, II.10. The song was a favourite from *c.* 1810.

Sir Walter Scott (1771–1832)

The Lay of the Last Minstrel (1805), Canto II Fanny quotes lines from II.10 and 12 to express her disappointment that Sotherton chapel is not gloomy or melancholy (*Mansfield Park*, I.9). Later, as she is sent off from the ball by Sir Thomas, stops 'like the lady of Branxholme Hall, "one moment and no more", [Lay, I. 20] to view the happy scene' (*Mansfield Park*, II.10). Most of the notes are derived from Scott's own.
Canto II **39 aventayle:** helmet visor. **60 drie:** perpetual. **130 Scottish monarch:** Alexander II. **377 litherly:** idle. **411 cushat-dove:** wood-pigeon or ring-dove.

Marmion (1808) JA asks in a letter of 20 June 1808, 'Ought I to be very much pleased with Marmion? – as yet I am not. – James reads it aloud in the evening'; and the poem is mentioned in *Persuasion*, I.11, where Captain Benwick wonders 'whether Marmion or The Lady of the Lake were to be preferred'. More specifically, JA's letter of 29 January 1813 parodies *Marmion*, 6.38 in connection with *Pride and Prejudice*, which has just come out: 'There are a few Typical errors – and a "said he" or a "said she" would sometimes make the Dialogue more immediately clear but "I do not write for such dull elves/As have not a great deal of ingenuity themselves" '; and in *Sanditon*, ch. 7, Sir Edward quotes the first line of *Marmion*, 6.30 to the long-suffering Charlotte, commenting 'Delicious! Delicious! – Had he written nothing more, he would have been immortal.' **13 runnel:** rivulet. **38 brand:** sword.

The Lady of the Lake (1810) Sir Edward quotes the first two lines of stanza 22 as 'that unequalled, unrivalled address to Parental affection'; a letter of 6 June 1811 concerning pea-picking says: 'our gatherings are very small – not at all like the Gathering in the Lady of the Lake' (which seems to refer to canto II.17, ll.7–12; though Le Faye suggests it might also be to III.24). **2 pibroch:** martial bagpipe tune. **66 shallop:** dinghy.

Robert Southey (1774–1843)

The Poet's Pilgrimage to Waterloo (1816) In her letter dated 24 January 1817 to Alethea Bigg, JA writes: 'We have been reading the "Poet's Pilgrimage to Waterloo," and generally with much approbation. Nothing will please all the world, you know; but parts of it suit me better than much that he has written before. The opening – the *Proem* I believe he calls it – is very beautiful. Poor man! One cannot but grieve for the loss of the Son so fondly described.'

James Thomson (1700–48)

The Seasons (1730; final form, 1746); *Spring* (1746 edn) ll.1113 to end. Ll.1152–3 are slightly misquoted in *Northanger Abbey*, I.1, in the list of virtues a heroine requires. **35 blows:** blooms.

William Whitehead (1715–85)

The Je ne scai quoi In Dodsley (see **Browne** above), II.265–6. Stanza 1 is quoted in *Mansfield Park*, II.12: Henry Crawford is 'determined to marry Fanny Price' and ' "How the pleasing plague had stolen on him" he could not say'; and is paraphrased in *Volume the Second*, A Collection of Letters, Letter the Fifth: 'on a sudden he interrupted me in the midst of something I was saying, by exclaiming in a most theatrical tone – 'Yes I'm in love I feel it now/ And Henrietta Halton has undone me" ' (*Minor Works*, ed. R. W. Chapman (London: Oxford University Press, 1969), p.167).